TO THE PERFORMER

A guide to the singer/songwriter for performance and other stage techniques

Amy Speace / Windbone
Nashville, Tennessee

First Edition
Published by Amy Speace / Windbone
www.amyspeace.com

ACKNOWLEDGMENTS

To my teachers from Williamsport High School choir director to Mr. Gallup to Jimmy Tripp at the National Shakespeare Conservatory, Cecily Barry from the Royal Shakespeare Company, to Janis Ian, Kathy Mattea and Julie Portman, performance teachers extraordinaire who really encouraged me to keep teaching. And Vance Gilbert, singer/songwriter/comedian/ performance teacher, who swears I stole everything from him. And The Rocky Mountain Folks Festival Song School, Kerrville Folk Festival Song School and Swannannoa Gathering for offering me a place to work out this method. Mostely to my students, for bringing your talent and vulnerability to the stage.

Lastly, to all of the record labels in NYC who told me I'd never have a career.

This book is for anyone who aspires to be or already is on the path to become a Performing Singer-Songwriter. It also applies to singers who don't do their own original material, jazz singers, musical theater and opera singers. The techniques come from acting techniques but apply across the board to ALL performers. I'd venture to say, as well, public speakers and lecturers could translate all the 'folk singer/songwriter' language to encompass their oeuvre.

CONTENTS

INTRODUCTION

You may have picked this book up because you've taken my classes. Or because the title seemed up your alley and you have no idea who I am. Even my students don't really know my whole history and how I came to knowing what I know and teaching what I know. So an introduction, I feel, is necessary.

Over the past twenty years, I've been teaching weeklong performance classes to singer/songwriters at various music festival songwriting camps. I began teaching and developing my class at The Rocky Mountain Folks Festival Song School in Lyons, Colorado. I was asked to step in for the long-time teacher, who had recently been diagnosed with cancer. The director of the program, Steve Szymanski, approached me the night before school was to begin. He said, "Can you put together a four-day comprehensive performance class?" I didn't hesitate, "Yes, of course," I said. When he left, I panicked. I thought: why did I say yes? I'm in over my head. I'd never taught anything to anyone.

I'd been a touring and recording singer-songwriter myself for years. I knew how to perform, but I wasn't sure how to teach it. But, the way the universe works, an idea came to me in a flash and, over the course of a few years of teaching, a methodology formed based on my years studying acting. You see, before I ever wrote a song, I was in theater.

After college, I moved to New York City, to study at The National Shakespeare Conservatory for their two-year professional acting certificate. I then went on to work in mostly classical theater for five years, became part of a repertory theater that produced "Shakespeare in the Park(ing) Lot." Did other rep theater. Toured the country for a year in The National Shakespeare Company. I wrote plays and co-founded and was the Artistic Director of the off-off Broadway, Five Points Theater Company. There, I put together workshops for schools in the neighborhood and created an apprentice program for those kids. I was twenty-five years old, hungry and ballsy and I talked my way into being invited to use a black box theater space at the Abrons Arts Center in the Lower East Side. They invited us to also be umbrellaed into their not-for-profit status, allowing us to apply for grants. To be honest, I look back at that girl with awe. She pretty much talked her way into everything. But I learned how to teach acting to kids, while taking master classes in acting myself.

My greatest teacher was Cecily Barry, the voice and diction coach for the Royal Shakespeare Company in London. She taught me how to speak Shakespearean lines as if they were thoughts popping up in real time. She taught me how to understand the language and the syntax and speak it as though I were just conversing with someone in my own life. I began to understand what "To be or not to be..." really meant and it helped me with choosing which word to emphasize, based on both the pentameter rhythm (and breaks in the pentameter), and the sense of the line.

That night, before I had to teach, I thought about what I've seen in young singer-songwriters. I'd studied with brilliant teachers who explained the techniques of performing. Where to stand in relation to the microphone. How to walk onstage. If the key was right for the performer, etc. But I'd seen no teacher address the internal workings of the performer. I've seen countless singer-songwriters oversell the song. I've seen countless "shoe gazers." I know when I hear someone and I *believe* them, even if the song is not autobiographical. I started to think about *how* to guide performers to connect to their own songs in a radical way, to deepen their relationship with their material without head waggling, over gesturing or pushing the performance into musical theater territory. I wanted something real, in the moment, not rehearsed, not canned. How to teach that?

I went back to how Cecily taught us to speak Shakespeare in the moment. She said to us, you're asking yourself two main questions of the character speaking the text:

1. Who are you talking to?
2. What are you trying to do *to* them or get *from* them?

I stayed up all night thinking of exercises and ways to guide my fellow students (because, basically, I was a student until Steve asked me to teach) to connect in a more honest way with their audience.

And then, I winged it.

Over the last twenty years, I've developed what I teach into a methodology that I've watched work over and over. I simply ask the questions, then offer scenarios in order that the performer is coming to their material in the *now*, not in the moment of writing. It doesn't really matter who the performer wrote the song about or to whom if the performer isn't currently connecting to it in the moment of the performance. So I throw different possibilities their way based on hearing the lyric of the song and the TRUTH the song is asking of them as performer.

I've watched magical transformations happen over and over. I credit all of this to Cecily and my years acting in classical productions. Song is like verse. It is syntactically different from regular speech, so we need to come to it singing it like we'd say it. I use improvisation, I borrow from The Meisner acting method. And I wing it.

I've seen it work time and time again. I credit the bravery and honesty of my students with helping me develop this course. In this book, I explain the method. I also want this book to inspire performers and give some practical tools. I feel like the method of performance and some of the tools can work beyond just a singer-songwriter, and could crossover to work for public speakers, poetry readings, etc.

Thank you for picking this book up and reading it and let's begin the journey!

Chapter One

HOW IT HAPPENED FOR ME

I've written this chapter in order to tell my own story and give you a bit of context as to where I'm coming from as a teacher and as a performer. It's my 'origin story.' We all have them. We can look back on our lives and see how each celebration, each failure has gotten us right exactly where we're supposed to be. I see that now for myself, even though if you'd have asked me in my twenties where I was headed, I would have told you I was lost. Here's the story and how I got here, making a living as a folk/americana singer-songwriter who tours the world and makes a decent living from it, under the 'fame' radar.

I started playing piano by ear when I was three years old, but nobody would take me for lessons until I was five. Lessons killed my ability to hear melodies and plunk them out and for the next decade I took the standard piano lessons, never practiced, learned to sight read and fool my teachers (I think), which made for a very mediocre piano player, but a *great* sight reader. I started studying clarinet in fourth grade and by the end of the year the teacher told me he was going to kick me out of band for not being any good (of course, I never practiced). That summer, I doubled down and took lessons and learned to practice. When I got back to school in the fifth grade, I found out I was a musician. Not only was I able to stay in band, I was given solos. I was hooked on music. By seventh grade I was first chair in the band and very serious about the clarinet.

I joined choir that year with my best friend Laura—mostly because we were the class clowns, making up skits and making people laugh and we were addicted to attention. I loved acting and being onstage and had been doing community theater productions of non-musicals in town, but the only way onstage in our Middle School was through the end-of-the-year choir musical review. So Laura and I joined. Neither of us thought of ourselves as good singers. But I secretly wanted nothing more than to be a GREAT singer. I was obsessed with the soundtrack to *Annie*, and I'd practice singing along to that soundtrack every day after school. Little did I know that practicing that hard turned me into a real singer. By the time the end of the year musical review came around, Mr. Douglas offered me a solo doing "Adeleide's Lament" from *Guys and Dolls*. He told me he gave it to me because I did a perfect New York accent (from my joking around with accents in class), which to me meant that he didn't give it to me because of my singing voice. Another music teacher from another middle school would come over after school and work with those of us who wanted extra help. I loved her and she heard something in me that nobody else had so far. She heard a singer. She encouraged me to start to really study voice outside of school and suggested a teacher and I signed up for lessons that summer.

The night of the review, I was nervous. The auditorium was standing room only. Laura had a solo too. Marissa DeSalvo was the star of our choir along with Todd Griffith. They both had vibratos and lovely voices. I longed to have a vibrato and be a "real" singer. But I knew I could make people laugh and "Adeleide's Lament" was a crowd pleaser. I remember my father driving me to the school that evening and he asked me if I was nervous (he told this story well into my adulthood). I replied, "Not at all. I can't WAIT to get up on that stage."

I crushed it. I got a standing ovation. Everyone went to my parents to tell them I should actually do this. That I was really talented. A star performer. Onstage, I honestly feel like I found myself. I was a good student, but not the best. I studied and practiced the clarinet, but I hadn't figured out what made me special yet. I wrote stories, but others were much better. There were the star mathematicians. There were the popular girls, the cheerleaders, the gymnasts who won medals. I felt average. Until that night. Onstage, singing that song, I found out who I wanted to be more than anything. I wanted to be a performer. An actor, a singer, it didn't matter. I wanted to live onstage.

And so I did throughout high school. I was blessed to go one of our country's top public school district music programs (we got an award for it from the Disney Foundation while I was a senior). I got solos in choir. I sang in the show choir and got the lead or the second lead in every years' musicals. My senior year I played Maria in *West Side Story*. My friends were in awe that I cried real tears. I went all Method Acting. I studied with a voice teacher who had gone to Julliard. I spent the summer after my junior year at The Pennsylvania Governor's School for the Arts, which took six singers (and actors and dancers and visual artists and musicians) out of thousands that had auditioned, and gave us a summer arts immersion experience. My vocal teacher, Diana, told me I was something special and encouraged me to audition for Eastman School of Music to major in vocal performance to be a classical singer.

I went back to high school for my senior year and worked hard at my audition for conservatory's. But I was torn, because I was also an A or B student and I was obsessed with being a writer. I wrote plays and stories and bad, bad poetry. My parents, not having any experience with a life in the arts, were quietly steering me to liberal arts colleges, so while I was auditioning for Eastman, I was writing essays for Amherst College, Middlebury, Williams.

The day came when Eastman called to offer me a full scholarship. I told them I wasn't sure what to do because I wanted to be a writer as well. They offered to accept me in a joint program with the University of Rochester to be get a BA in English and a BS in Music for a special five-year program. Fully funded. I was elated.

The next week came my acceptance from Amherst, a prestigious "Little Ivy" college in Massachusetts that looked like the brochure for the perfect New England college. I was torn.

I went to the liberal arts college in my hometown to talk to the head of the music department there. We'd met a few times, and he knew of my singing. I asked him for advice. He said, "If you can do anything well besides music, do that. Music is a very hard path." I didn't want to be a music teacher and I knew that was my option if I didn't "make it" as an opera or classical singer. I also wanted to have the typical New England college experience with football games and bon fires and keggers and a capella singing groups. I didn't want to walk around dirty Rochester with a scarf around my neck to protect my precious singing voice for four (or five) years.

I chose Amherst. I did study classical voice all throughout college. I started out as a music major but hated theory. I'd taken an acting class for fun (and to give me something a bit easier than Critical Theory, James Joyce Seminar and all the heavy-reading classes I'd taken on). I was hooked. I remembered why I loved being onstage. I was an ACTOR! I also joined the a capella group and so I was able to scratch the singing/acting/comedy itch through those shows. It also, strangely gave me instant popularity (if you've been to one of those colleges, you know what I mean). I was in every musical production on campus. I wrote plays. I directed plays. I ended up a double major in English and Theater, writing two thesis for double honors . I studied jazz piano as an extra elective, and, since I'd been studying voice so thoroughly, I also did a senior recital, singing arias and chansons and a few vocal jazz numbers. I was so diversified, that leading up to graduation I had zero idea what I was going to do with my life. My peers were headed to medical and law School or off to get PhD's in Comparative Literature from Harvard and Yale. I hadn't thought of my future. I took my two favorite English professors out to lunch one day, one of whom was my thesis advisor. I asked them if they'd give me recommendations for a PhD program in English (I was graduating magna cum laude so I was no academic slouch). They both said no. "We don't know what you should or will be doing, but you should just go to New York. You should be on stage. You should be singing. If nothing happens in five years, we'll write you recommendations." (Believe me, I have thanked both of them over and over for refusing me entrance into academia).

Peter Lobdell, a Theater professor of mine, taught every summer at The National Shakespeare Conservatory's Summer Program and invited me to go there. It was a ten-week immersion on a camp in the Catskills. We'd wake at seven in the morning and study ballet and movement. We worked with a voice coach from the Royal Shakespeare Company in London. We studied Shakespeare, we did scenes, we learned monologues. I was hooked. After that summer, I was accepted into their two-year Conservatory Program for Classical Acting in New York City that fall.

I deferred school to work for a year to earn money to move to New York. I stayed in Amherst and lived with a rock band (my boyfriend was the lead singer). I worked at a bakery in town. I rode my bike through the mountains. I worked with Peter on some avant-garde dance/theater pieces (I hated them—I wasn't a dancer) and I studied voice every week in New York City, travelling by train back and forth every Thursday. I did a fair amount of mushrooms and smoked a lot of weed and thought about starting a punk band too. It was a wild ride of a year, but I was ready to start my life in earnest, and that summer I got a job at The Weston Theater in Vermont, a summer stock theater company. I was humbled as I got no speaking roles, no solos. I was just in the chorus. The leads were all from "real" acting schools, they all lived in New York and already had impressive resumes. I was the newbie. I realized I wasn't that good. I had a decent voice, but not necessarily a musical theater voice. I again stumbled in my self-awareness. No matter, I was headed to Manhattan in September to study classical acting. I'd be a Shakespearean actress and not do musicals anymore.

For two years I got my ass kicked at the Conservatory. It was like clarinet. I wasn't that good. The other students were more seasoned. But I had a champion in Mark Zeller, the voice and speech coach, who saw something in me and invited me to study privately with him over the summer. He worked me hard twice a week and by the end of the summer, I was a real actress. I came back to Conservatory for the second year a different person. I KNEW I wanted to do this and I was good.

But I'd given up singing. At that point, at 22 years old, I hadn't written a song. I didn't play guitar. I wasn't a pop singer. I wasn't a jazz singer (although I'd tried to be in college). My voice didn't really fit doing current musical theater (belters), so I stopped singing. After I graduated, I got the three requisite jobs to live in NYC and pay rent while hopping from audition to audition. I auditioned for musicals and would get called back until the dance call and be stuck in a room with thin, tall women in leotards and Capezio shoes, while I was there in shorts and socks. I failed every musical audition I did. I just wasn't a "chorus girl" and I didn't have the resume to be considered for a lead role. So, I did off and off-off Broadway classical pieces. Oh, I loved those days. I worked as a temporary paralegal at law firms. I was the actress Lainie Kazan's personal assistant for many years and got to work with her on Broadway. I bartended for two nights. I got fired as a waiter when I spilled wine on someone while trying to uncork the bottle. I lived in the Village and spent my free times hanging out at cafes writing in my journals, meeting up with artists and directors and actors and poets and dancers. It was exactly what I'd always wanted: to be immersed in Bohemia. I'd find my way, I thought, eventually. But for now, I live in Greenwich Village and I'm acting in New York City.

By the time I was twenty-eight, nothing had changed. I couldn't get an agent. I was still floundering in secondary parts. I couldn't catch a break. I started looking back into graduate schools. I even looked into going to law School. At the time, my boyfriend the rock star was touring the country on the verge of his band being signed to a major label. I loved watching him up there, the lead singer of a band, writing his own songs. I remembered when I was younger, around sixteen years old, studying piano. My parents would be out. Nobody would be home and I'd light candles at the piano and hover my hands above the keys, thinking that you wrote songs by praying to God to move your hands. I wrote a nice easy instrumental piece. Then forgot it a month later. I gave up. I had a crush on the senior in high school who was a songwriter. I dated songwriters my whole life. Now I had come to understand— I didn't want to date them—I wanted to BE them.

Just by virtue of being around the rock star, I learned a few guitar chords. All I needed was three and I put some of my journal writing to music, made up a melody, and had my first song, "Lovely." I still remember the chorus. It soared. It had promise. The lyrics went nowhere, it was just a love song: "I remember this—that you were lovely." That's all I remember about it, but it leapt up an octave on "I – Re" and I loved singing it. I wrote another song. Tried to play it for the rock star, but he was busy being a rock star and just said, "yeah yeah, babe, that's cool." And went back to smoking the bowl.

We had a spectacular break up, involving a beautiful boy named Paul, a tab of ecstasy, a closing night party and then finding out he'd cheated on me for years. I was living in an apartment with three guys, one of them was Paul, and it became evident that I had to leave. So, I crashed on a friend's couch for a month, bought a Seagull guitar for $300, listened to Tori Amos' *Little Earthquakes* over and over and proceeded to write ten songs. Bad songs, but ten songs. Writing the songs was hard, but when I was done and I could sing them back to myself, I had that same feeling I had onstage performing "Adeleide" in middle school. I knew who I was. I couldn't get enough of it.

I was invited by a friend to play a few songs during his gig at The Bitter End, a famed folk club on Bleecker Street in the West Village. I was afraid to do it alone, so I called my friend from college Erin Ash to sing harmonies. She sang with me in the a capella group at Amherst. "I've been writing songs, too," she said, and we practiced a set of duo songs, two hers, two mine. At the end of our short set, Kenny, the booker for the club, came up and offered us a gig. "What's the name of your band?" We said, "We'll get back to you on that one."

We named ourselves Edith of Ohio, after a nineteenth century wild child. We ended up shortening it to Edith O. and became fixtures at The Bitter End and the acoustic clubs in New York and developed a following. It was the era of Lilith Fair and The Indigo Girls were hot. We were both five foot four, blonde, with short hair. We sang well. We wrote hooky pop songs and both played acoustic guitar. We had great harmonies. Soon, we had major labels sniffing around, taking us out for expensive dinners, giving us their cell phone numbers. We had a big time lawyer. We were on the verge of something.

With the help of financial backers (and our parents), we made a record, *Tattooed Queen* with a band. We booked a release show on a Saturday night at The Bitter End. Erin had gotten married while we were recording, and then became pregnant. She also worked as an elementary school teacher and loved it. Her husband was a comic and a comedic writer, always traveling to LA. I worried about her commitment, but she kept telling me she was "in".

It came the night of our CD Release Show. The band was there. I was there. Erin was not. It came time to get onstage. I asked Kenny to hold the show for five minutes. I called Erin from the house phone (pre-cell phone era). "Hi," she said. "Hey, what are you doing?" I asked, gritting my teeth. "Oh, just baking cookies, what are you doing?" "I'm at the CD Release Show waiting for you." She'd forgotten.

I can say it took a few years for us to get back to speaking after that, but these days we are really close and, at 55 years old, Erin made a CD of her music after giving it up for decades, and she's the new toast of the folk world and I couldn't be prouder of her.

That night, I told Kenny, "Erin's not coming. Half the set is her songs and I don't know them." He said, "Welcome to your solo career, kid." And I went onstage terrified and played half the set. I don't remember that night. I wanted to crawl under the Brooklyn Bridge. There were managers and A&R people from labels in the audience there to see the new hot duo. And they saw me, in my first solo show, completely unprepared to hold the whole show. I bombed.

I tried to follow up with the A&R people but they said they were most interested in the duo but, did I have a demo of my solo work? I had just spent all that money on a CD with Erin and so, no, I didn't. They thanked me and moved on. So, I quit. I took the next acting gig I got and immersed myself again in theater.

A manager that had been interested in Edith O. called me one day to ask where I'd gone. I told him what had happened. He said he wouldn't let me quit. At the time, he was a manager and an A&R rep at Shanachie Records, a Celtic folk label. He asked me, "have you been writing?" I said, "yes." He said, come over and we'll make a tape of every song you've written. I began to work with him on my songs. He told me to practice with a metronome, so that once I played with a drummer I could hold a steady groove. He taught me song form. He got me shows at places I couldn't get shows before with Erin. He pulled in favors. He believed in me. Matt MacHaffie. I am forever grateful to him. I can honestly say I'm here still because of Matt. He pushed me to be an artist, not just a girl with a guitar on stage who sang pretty.

He also introduced me to artists from out of town, who would come to NYC to play shows. One of them invited me to come to Albany to share a show with him. It was my first "tour" of two shows. I slept on his couch— made no money and had a blast. Matt taught me to start out touring, doing three-day concentric circles of shows. Albany, Syracuse, home. Connecticut, Boston, home. He said take every show you get. Every unpaid chance to sing in front of an audience and I don't care if it's in the dementia unit of a nursing home, you take it. You need practice. I did that. The Albany artist invited me on a real tour with him. He was driving and playing his way to Wisconsin and back and wanted to know if I'd share the show with him, which was incredibly generous because he'd booked them all himself. We'd sleep on couches. I said, absolutely!

Then 9/11 happened. Our tour was set for October. We decided to still do it, hoping that people wanted to hear music during that time. We played cafes and colleges, the early shows at some rock clubs. We played Cincinnati to Milwaukee. Some of the people and bookers I met on that tour are still in my life.

Something shifted in me watching the Towers fall (I watched the whole event on the banks of the Hudson River from Hoboken, NJ in shock and counting all the people I knew who worked in the Center...none of them were lost). It gutted me (and everyone else, of course) and I viscerally felt life was short. I made a decision at that moment that I was going to have a life as a singer-songwriter, that I would tour, that I would make records, no matter the money. If I had to sustain three McJobs, I would. I wanted it that badly. I would go to Songwriting Camps and learn to write. I'd listen to the best songwriters. I'd study the art. I'd work on my vibrato-laden voice. I'd learn to put a show together.

That tour, on top of 9/11, started my career. I booked another in the summer with another friend from NYC for seven weeks across to California and back. I'd figured out the college booking system (they paid real money and got you a hotel), and I could talk our way into clubs in LA by just saying we were from NYC. I had a tiny write-up in which was my only press, but it opened some doors. That tour was my master class. My voice was pitchy before that tour, always a bit flat. My leg shook on stage. For someone who'd studied acting, being on stage with just my songs and my guitar was terrifyingly vulnerable for me. But by the time I got back, after having played almost every night of that tour, I had learned this job. My voice wasn't pitchy. My leg stayed still and I'd written a handful of new songs.

Matt suggested I work with a few musicians he knew from the scene and I started to put together more songs. John Abbey, a renowned bass player in NYC had just built a recording studio in his Williamsburg, Brooklyn loft and we decided to make a record. A friend loaned me $5,000. We hired a drummer and a guitar player and finished the record, but I sat on it because I didn't have the money to put it out.

Around that time, I was walking to the subway from my loft in Hoboken that I shared with four other people and noticed that the local flower shop on first avenue was being turned into a guitar store and there was a guy with a porkpie hat in the window hanging guitars. I walked in and boldly introduced myself as a neighborhood musician. He was kind. Asked me what I played. I told him I played guitar and that I was a songwriter. He asked if I had a demo. I had just written this new song that hadn't made the record and I had a tape of it and gave it to him. That night I went to see The Jayhawks in concert. That guy in the porkpie hat was onstage with them playing accordion and singing. The next day I walked into his shop and asked him "Who ARE you?? I'm a huge Jayhawks fan...I saw you last night." Turns out it was James Mastro, who was a New Jersey (and NYC) legend. He'd played with Television when he was sixteen. He had an acclaimed early alt-country band called The Health and Happiness Show. He was the real deal. James asked me what I was working on. I told him I'd just recorded an album but it was sitting around. He asked if this song was on it. No, I said. And he offered to produce it for me to put on the record. James was also an acclaimed producer. I knew none of this. I had just walked into a flower shop.

A few months later, I was playing a showcase for The Songwriter's Hall of Fame. I'd been invited by my BMI rep, and a man (we'll call him Steve) introduced himself to me. He asked me why he didn't know of me. Where had I been? I said, I'm right here, slogging away in folk clubs in New York City, laughing. He asked me if I'd ever gone to the International Folk Alliance Conference. I had never even heard of it. Within a week, he'd paid for me to reproduce my album, then called *Fable*, and paid for my registration and hotel room for the Folk Alliance that was in Jacksonville that year. I had no idea what I was going into when I entered that hotel. It seemed like thousands of musicians, playing in the lobby, schmoozing, managers and booking agents and small folk labels, festival bookers, accordion players in the elevator and posters announcing "showcases" everywhere. Tom, the man who was my patron, had gotten me one 'showcase', basically a fifteen-minute set in a hotel bedroom at 1am that night. Again: it was all so foreign to me I just went with the flow, completely naïve.

I tell the rest of this story in the chapter on *Gigs*. It changed my life. So much serendipity was involved, but I was ready for it.

Around this time, I'd taken my record to all the Major Labels in New York to try to get a demo deal. They used to give these out to emerging artists where they'd invest in making demos and to see if the artist was good enough to invest in a full-length record. Every door that opened closed when they'd all say, "Your songs are good but your voice...it sounds too much like Joan Baez and Judy Collins. You will never have a career in this business." I was disheartened but something had happened at the Folk Alliance to give me courage to continue.

A year later, I had been invited by another artist, Troy Campbell, who I'd met on tour in North Carolina, to come to the South by Southwest Music Festival in Austin to do an offshoot showcase at Threadgills Restaurant. He said, "I can only give you fifteen minutes." I was to play before Gurf Morlix, who I knew of because he had produced Lucinda Williams, one of my idols. In the audience happened to be Katherine DePaul, Judy Collins' manager, who had just started a record label for Judy and was sent to the show to investigate Gurf as a potential signee. But Judy had told Katherine, "Try to find a young version of me." Katherine asked me for a demo, not telling me who she was. I gave her a copy of a new series of recordings I was making with James, to be my second record. I went home feeling like I'd wasted a lot of money to go to Austin and got nothing out of it.

A few weeks later, I got a call from Katherine, introducing herself to me as Judy Collins' manager and label president, and that Judy loved my record and wanted to sign me and put the record out as is and would I be able to fly to Minnesota that weekend to open for Judy at a theater. After being told I'd never have a career because I sounded too much like Judy Collins, it was unbelievable to me that it was Judy herself that found me.

I'll just say life changed drastically. I was touring the country, opening shows for Judy. I was being invited to play at international showcases for Judy's label distributors. I met Jack Holzman who had originally signed Judy to Electra in the 1960s. When I went back to the Folk Alliance the next year, there was a buzz and my showcases were packed. Festivals that had walked past my door while I was playing the year prior booked me on the spot. I got a booking agent (Sean had passed away by then). The generous patron, had started a management company and became my manager and had hired a woman to be my 'day to day' person. I was touring the country with my band with financial backing. I was getting reviewed in major magazines. People began to know who I was. It was magic.

But here's the thing. It was part coincidence and part hard work. A LOT of hard work. Someone once said to me, "You have to work twice as hard to become a great songwriter because you're a good singer. You want to be a singer SONGWRITER. You don't want the first thing people say to you as you walk off stage to be 'what a great singer you are'. You want them to say 'what a great songwriter you are. Oh, and also, your voice is great.'"

So, I doubled down on writing. I began making trips to Nashville to write with anyone I'd meet. I met the Grammy Award winning songwriter Jon Vezner at a songwriting camp at which he was teaching. He liked my songs and invited me to come to Nashville to co-write with him. I cancelled my plans, quit my McJob, and drove to Nashville the next week and spent a week drinking coffee and writing songs with Jon. Through Jon I met a slew of other incredible songwriters who offered to write with me.

Fast forward a few years and I was having some issues with Wildflower Records (Judy's label) who were dragging their feet putting out my 2009 release, *The Killer In Me*. I randomly met the president of the indie label service company, Thirty Tigers on a plane. We hit it off talking about music and books. I told him I had a record being held up. That night he googled me and listened to some of my music. I again ran into him by complete accident the next day and he said he had been looking for me, that he loved my music and that he wanted to work with me. David Macias became my manager and signed me to Thirty Tigers that year. That was the January. He introduced me to publishers and writers who all said, "you belong in Nashville." So, I moved to Nashville in September 2009. My record came out but got lost in the shuffle. David introduced me to Neilson Hubbard, a producer whose work I knew already. I was a fan of his production style. We began writing together which turned into making recordings of those songs, which turned into my first Nashville record, *Land Like a Bird*, which Thirty Tigers put out in 2011.

I left Thirty Tigers in 2014. I'd put out two records with them, including *How To Sleep in a Stormy Boat*, which landed me on Weekend Edition on NPR. Through Thirty Tigers, I'd met publicists and photographers and radio promoters and when David stepped down from managing me, he connected me with my current manager John Porter. We put a team together of our own, and found our own funding, and have put out records through my own label with national distribution ever since. My records have been on labels outside the US, I own my own masters and I've toured internationally.

I've made a living for over twenty years doing this. Once I left NYC to move to Nashville, I didn't need to have a sustenance job. Music was one-hundred percent paying my bills. The cost of living (at that time, Nashville had gotten stupid expensive) was significantly lower in Nashville, so you could make a decent living as a touring folk/americana singer. But I've had highs and lows as you've read. I quit many times. I still quit in my head. I make a living, I own my own house, I can pay my bills, but I don't have much wiggle room. I have a son now and I don't like the idea of hustling the rest of my life without some padding of money. I quit all the time. And then I'm onstage and I'm extremely grateful for the hundred, or fifty, or ten people that have paid twenty-five dollars and taken a few hours out of their life to come hear me sing my songs and tell my stories. I love my job. I love my life. It's been a lot of hard work.

I've had a lot of angels along the way, from my college professors to James Mastro, to my patron, to Judy Collins, to Jon Vezner, to David Macias of Thirty Tigers, to my current manager. Doors have opened and I've just walked through them not questioning. I've never had a five-year plan. I've never had a backup plan. I just kept working really hard to be the best songwriter I could be. It's why I moved to Nashville, to 'up my game.' Nashville is a master class in songwriting. There's something in the water.

I've had doors slammed in my face and I've stuck with it. I'm either really determined or I'm stupid. I have no 401K plan. That first agent, Sean LaRoche? I paid him $300 a month to book me because I knew fifteen percent of what I was going to make wasn't going to be worth his time. My current manager? During Covid when I wasn't working and he wasn't making any money off me, I paid him $500 a month to stick with me. That's wasn't easy. I don't make THAT much money. But I needed him and he's been my partner in this venture for the last ten years.

When people ask me how I did it, I say it's a long story. When they say, "I want to do what you do," I want to encourage them NOT to quit their jobs ... yet. The music industry was a different beast back then. It was the beginning of the internet. MySpace was the only social media. Not everyone was making records in their home studios. You could still cut through the noise. It's harder these days. I just say to people what I was told: "Concentrate on writing the best songs you can. A great song cuts through and will carry you." I can say "The Killer in Me" was the first song that got me though the noise. "The Sea and the Shore" got me on NPR. "Me and the Ghost of Charlemagne" won the 2020 International Song of the Year from the UK Americana Awards. Each one of those songs won me more fans, got me more money from venues, introduced me to more and more amazing writers.

If you want to do this, write. Write. Write. Take every gig offered to you. There's no one way to do this. Some people come out of the womb as genius writers. Some people write for decades until that ONE song comes. The song that teaches them their "Writer's Voice". My song was "Haven't Learned a Thing" that's on *The Killer In Me*. When I wrote that song I knew I'd found my 'voice'. Every song after that I held up to that song. I still do. I have those songs. My benchmark songs. I write a lot of crappy songs in order to get to the one I'll record.

Be careful of critics. Don't play your brand-new babies for just anyone. There are two people I play my new songs to. I don't want too many cooks in the kitchen and those are the two I trust that know my style and will comment having my best interest in mind rather than trying to make my song "hookier" or more commercial.

And practice. I say this to myself as much as you. Write the song and then practice it until you can play it live without looking at your guitar, without lyrics.

And always, always stay a beginner.

So, all the waving in the wind of my career? I can look back and now see the pattern that would only lead me here. Performing, teaching performance and songwriting and writing.

Find your passion and follow it. It will happen if it's meant to happen and if not, it will lead you to what your mission in life will be. We all make a difference in this world, in our own way. Just stop knocking on closed doors. Walk through the ones that are open.

Chapter Two

THE METHOD

Performing a song in front of anyone, whether it's our friends, the local open mic, or to an audience of three hundred can be thrilling and terrifying at the same time. How is it that some people make performing look easy? How do they not seem nervous? How do they look like they belong up there?

Yeah, ok. Some people came out of the womb comfortable onstage. Like, maybe, twenty-five people. Seriously. Not that many. Most of the people you see who *seem* like they've never known stage fright in their life either have learned how to live with it and work around it, or they've learned techniques to distract themselves from fear. Fear is like death and taxes – you can't wish it away. You just make friends with it and make it part of your team. You USE fear.

The thing is, GREAT performers don't forget they're onstage; they are fully aware (maybe more so) of being onstage, which brings a heightened awareness of their intention, their *mission*. They aren't just walking onstage in their street clothes, or comfy sweats (with the great exception of the brilliant Cheryl Wheeler), having just brushed their teeth, the stage and performance an afterthought. There is homework on performance. There is thought and research and there are choices to be made. Great performers have enough respect for the stage and for their audience that they prepare so they can adapt so they can fly.

In this world of the singer-songwriter, we can make the mistake of believing our Great Song will be so perfect and unique that it will move the masses and that we can just sing the words and play the guitar (oh, I forgot to practice an intro, so I'll just strum four bars of G and look at the ground or my hands) and our Great Lyric will pour into the ears of our audience, moving them to tears and change their lives. We don't realize that seventy-five percent of the time, the audience is bored after the second verse and has opened their Instagram feed because they are disconnected from you, the Great Writer, lost in an Average Performance.

If they don't receive the song, you have failed.

Performance is a different art than writing. You can be a great songwriter. You can be a great performer. Wouldn't it be amazing to be both? You practice songwriting. How do you practice performance? What would that look like besides just singing the song over and over again to your bedroom mirror in the clothes you'd wear onstage?

I believe being a performing songwriter isn't that different than being an actor in a play. Can you imagine an actor walking onto a Broadway stage, only knowing their lines, not having done any other work besides just remembering the lines? You can bet that's going to be a pretty static performance, one where the actor is "phoning it in". How many times in our own performances with our own songs have we found ourselves lost, disconnected, just singing the lyrics?

A well-written song, like a play, has a story. A beginning, middle and end. It has characters: the leading actor—the protagonist. The minor characters. Someone to whom the story is addressed (either real in the text or imagined by the performer). It has got a sense of place, scenery, props. You wrote it, right? You should know the story. But when it comes to performing the song, sometimes the REAL story of the song isn't that exciting to you anymore, you wrote it for that boyfriend seven years ago and you don't care anymore. Here's where you, as performer, can impose a new story on top of the same song to reconnect to seemingly dead material. It's the job of the performer to make choices about the story, from within the song and without. **The richer the choices, the richer your performance.**

Any song has Aristotelian elements of drama:

1. Plot – What happens in the song. What's going on here?
2. Theme – What's the whole song about?
3. Character – YOU in the song. Even if it's a 3rd person narrative who is that person who is singing the song? Are there other characters in the song?

4. Diction/language/dialogue – What kind of words are you using and how do they define you as the protagonist (star of the show)? Like are you country or urban? Low class? High class? Educated or uneducated?

5. Music/Rhythm – What is the groove and melody?

6. Spectacle— What's on stage with you when you sing?

Ok, so I know this may sound really academic, but I swear, it's useful. If you're lucky enough to have written a classic hit song that only needs you to stand up there and deliver it, and the audience is rendered powerless by the sheer amazingness of the lyrics and the music and your voice and your guitar playing every single time...well then, bless your damn lucky heart. But for the rest of us mere mortals, sometimes we have to dig a bit deeper to connect for whatever reason (you're tired; the food the promoter gave you sits heavy in our belly; it was a long drive; it's a new song; it's too old of a song; you're nervous because your college boyfriend is in the audience; your wife just yelled at you on the phone 5 minutes before you went onstage). The thing is: we all still have to perform, despite the obstacles.

When it's not as easy as just looking into the eyes of our adoring audience and sending them shivers of love and connection, how do we connect?

We ask questions of the song, utilizing any of the above elements to dig deeper, hopefully leading us inside the "story" of the song (or, in some cases *A* story of the song, "the story that will work tonight" of the song) and to find our way to the who what and why (and where) of the performance.

Why Do We Have To Do This? Isn't the Song Enough?

We do this because when you are booked to do a show where people are paying fifteen dollars a seat to be entertained, you don't have the luxury to just hope for an ON night. You have to deliver that. It is your job (and even if you're not getting anything but a percentage of the ticket fee, or it's an open mic, I challenge you to start performing as if everyone in the audience came specifically to see you and paid a lot of money for this chance).

Here's the key: It is not about YOU feeling something. It's about you opening THEM up to feel something.

Did you hear me?

The point of performance is not for the *performer* to be moved, but for the *audience* to be moved.

Nobody wants to see you cry. They want to cry themselves. (However, if you DO cry, and it's an honest moment, the trick is to breathe, let the emotion pass, but continue the work.)

This is the homework that you do on *Performance* that will seep into your skin and bones so that you have a technique to reach for when you're trying to glide along in the glow of a great performance, but realize it just ain't happening that night. A great performance is a wonderful thing: the FLOW of energy that is exchanged easily between audience and performer keeps the show exciting and alive. But sometimes it's not there. Sometimes you are playing to a theater full of people and you are blinded by the spotlight and all you can hear is whispering from the balcony and you feel entirely disconnected. You can't see them, you assume they don't like you, your internal critic gets louder in your head and you don't feel that juicy feeling you usually feel when you know you're hitting it out of the park.

Sometimes you're playing at a festival and you are way above and far away from the audience below, an audience of families throwing a beach ball around, enjoying the sunshine, picnicking, seemingly not paying attention to you. Sometimes you're playing to a loud bar full of rowdy people who just want to watch the TV above the bar, while you try like hell to connect to them with your sensitive sea shanties. Here's the thing: You. Still. Have. A. Show. To. Do. This is when it's a job. You show up.

Sometimes, you just have a bad night, an off night, you're in the middle of the song and you lose focus, you think of something in your own life that takes you out of the performance (your recent breakup, your late car payment, the traffic you just got stuck in and missed your soundcheck) and all of a sudden you're lost. We've all been there.

How do you get back? By checking back in with the following:

1. Who are you talking to?
2. What are you trying to do to them or get from them?

When you are lost or unfocused, before you start the song, you ask yourself these questions (just wait...I explain this soon). This will steady your nerves, put you in the song itself, into an active position, into the driver's seat and will pull you out of your own scattered, nervous mind. And you won't notice the hockey game on the TV set. You'll be focused on doing a job— doing a task—and, if successful, you will reach a few people who will be riveted. And they might even lose interest in the last half of the game. Change ONE person in that audience and the next time you play, they will bring five more friends to your next show. This isn't about being a huge star out of the box; it's by affecting your audience one person at a time.

Breaking Down The Song

Here's the secret of all of the stuff I'm about to write you below: Nobody except you needs to know your choices. You are about to do some role playing to find what works and what doesn't.

Who Are You?

This is for you to find out on your own. This is not part of the Method of Performance that I teach, but it will be helpful to you in terms of answering the two questions of the Method. In terms of you being the person performing this song, who is singing this song in the story? Who is the "I" and it was probably you when you wrote the song, but think about this now. Is the "I" young or old? Are they angry or sad? Where are they singing this physically from— in the bedroom or the boyfriend's house? Or the assumed "I" in the case of a he/she/them song. If it's not written into the song, make it up. Are you a person in love? Are you a mother? Are you a teacher? This is background work that an actor does. It just fills in your experience of the song, so you are not generating a vague performance.

What do you know about this story? Where has this story rung true for you? If you are the narrator, who are you to the he/she/them of the song? Are you their friend, brother, mother, lover, preacher, mayor, God? Make a choice. Try it out. See which choices give you tingles and new ideas and new things to do. Above all – play...

This question is the LEAST important question to be answered. Sometimes it becomes evident just by asking the next two questions and sometimes I don't even care who I am. I care more about who I'm talking to and what I'm trying to do to them than I do about myself. I'm me, always, on stage singing my songs. You will experience yourself through me if I'm doing my job well.

The Meat of the Method

These are the two essential questions I ask of a performer when I'm working with them in person. There are no right answers and they are provided to lead the performer to a true performance "in the now." We don't want to perform the song the same way over and over. Answering these questions keeps your performance interesting to you and fresh to the audience. Here we go:

Who Are You Talking To?

Who are you talking to in the song? If this a first-person song (the 'I') song, who is are you talking to? Are you talking to yourself? Or praying? For the sake of the Method, here are your choices:

1. A person. One person. Very specific. Like from-your-own-life specific. Like your mom. Your partner. Your boss.

2. Yourself. But you at a different age than you are right now. Either older or younger.

3. God (whatever that means to you).

So, let's break this down.

<u>One person</u>. Doesn't have to be the person you wrote the song about. In fact, if that person is now out of your life and does not have 'power' for you anymore, choose someone else. Substitute in your imagination someone who has power, energy, electricity for you, emotionally, NOW in your life. And by power I mean someone who evokes a strong reaction that is aligned with the emotional story of the song. You might have written the song to a lover who left you, begging them to come back. But maybe you want to explore what it would be like to sing this to your mother who never hugged you when you were

a kid. Or your roommate who never pays her share of the rent on time. Or your worst enemy. Or your boss. Truth should never get in the way of good fiction. What works from one day to the next might change. Feel free to explore.

Yourself. If the song is written to yourself, or for now you have made the choice to address yourself, I encourage you to address a You of a different age. Really spend some time thinking and imagining and then making real that You, real. Is that You, twelve? What are you wearing? What happened to you? Where are you? Visualize that twelve-year old in front of you and talk to them. Maybe you want to talk to the future: you in twenty years. How does that change the conversation?

God. ...and by God, I mean something outside of yourself, any higher power that works for you (it could be your God, it could be the trees, it could be a person who has died). Try making God a real person but someone who is no longer here. I always make God my grandmother, rocking in the black rocking chair in her maroon house coat, frayed at the sleeves, Kleenex sticking out of the sleeves, and the mismatched red and pink slippers, smelling of baby powder and lavender soap. When the choice is 'God' the need is a great, universal need. "From A Distance" is a good example of this kind of song. A big universal statement. 'God' in this case is the entire world. But how do you actually *envision* the entire population? You make it specific: humanize 'God'...my grandmother, a bird, a tree, the wind, etc. You can need something from the wind, from the birds, from anything. To be honest, the God you are addressing is really the same technique as #1, as addressing the song to one specific person from your life.

A word on saying "this song is being sung to a crowd," addressing a generic group of people, like audience, opens up the possibility of you just standing there BEING something, being IN a vague emotional state. *Feeling* the song. Which is to say, not really doing anything, just feeling something. Which is indulgent. Which isn't the point. That can seem really, really amateur. The audience doesn't want to see you "feeling" anything. They want to feel for themselves. Choose ONE person to sing to. Not "audience," not "crowd." If it's a "rousing the crowd" song, aim to inspire one person in that crowd.

"General" and "Vague" kill performances. General and Vague are our enemies. Be at constant battle with them.

What Are You Trying to Do *to* Them or Get *from* Them? (in other words: What's Your Intention?)

Now that you have figured out <u>who</u> you are talking to, <u>what</u> are trying to do? Are you trying to DO something TO that person or are you trying to GET something FROM them? How are you trying to change them? The doing of the thing is called the "action" or the "intention" of the moment/song/scene. This can be inherent in the song, or you can make an intention up that will accomplish the goal of deepening the performance for yourself in the moment.

Like I've said, in essence, you fire the songwriter while you're doing this work. If your ex doesn't make you want to plead with them anymore, choose someone else. You want to choose actions that are physical and strong and have some resonance for you. You might see that the song is all about a person pleading to another for love. In "I Can't Make You Love Me" of course, inherent in the lyric is someone sad about a relationship gone south. Does the singer want the relationship back or do they want to learn how to let it go? And maybe there's both in there. 'I want them to love me.' That is a bit vague. Deepen that with an Action. "I want them to hold me tonight for the last time." HOLD is more active than LOVE—you can do something with hold -- you can physicalize hold. How about, "I want them to wrap their arms around my waist and not let me go." That's active! What about "I want to root them to the ground so they'll stay through the night.' That is more active than "I don't want them to leave." So, let's choose "I want them to wrap his arms around my waist" but let's make that bigger, more dramatic. "I want them to pour their soul into my veins." Well, that's really big and very descriptive. It's metaphoric, but if you use your imagination... let's continue.

How do you do that? How would you do that? And how would you do that WITHOUT MOVING YOUR ARMS? It would come out in your voice, in your inflections, in your eyes. Mostly, it's in your gut. You *think* it. It takes a bit of practice and trust. You might choose to seduce. Or to comfort. Or to tickle. Or to beg. Or to demand. There are a thousand ways you could try to get this person to do this. How would you sing the line standing still as if you were stamping your feet like a little kid and demanding it? How would it feel and sound if you were, without moving away from the microphone, whispering in a lover's ear. Or singing the phrase as if you were wolf, circling your prey, your lover, without moving anything but your mouth.

The trick is to play. And the thing is with this stuff, it's metaphorical and it can all seem very wooshy gooshy new agey 'be a tree' kind of thing. But maybe, just maybe, try it. Try to imagine your words are slapping the person across the face (you don't DO anything physical and you don't push the voice out to 'slap'...it's a small shift and you will not move and your voice will not push it, but the audience will feel riveted).

Choose a line from your song and without doing anything with your body, say the line to either a real partner or an imagined person, and, with Intention, try to beg, or demand, or seduce. Each different action you choose produces a different way of speaking the line. Your experience of your own writing might change and the relationship you have to the line will deepen. Now try singing it with that change. Not over acting, not pushing too hard, but just with the truth of the Action.

Sometimes each verse is a different action, you are trying different ways of getting the same result, just as each verse should build on the next, changing the meaning of the chorus, or deepening it from verse to verse. Think of the song as a sailboat and you are the sail, choosing to change tacks with the wind. You might try to comfort in the first verse and then seduce in the second.

The thing is, you are not going to be changing the lyrics of the song, nor are you going to be showing or telling anything to the audience so that they will know what your Intent is, what your *action* choices are. They will simply experience a riveting performance.

Also, for the most part, I am a big fan of 'sing it like you'd say it' in terms of phrasing. I'll say a phrase from my lyric out loud and really hear the words I emphasize naturally. Then I'll check in with my melody line and make sure that I'm emphasizing the stress words in that melodic line. You don't want the top of your phrase in a long strongly held out belted note to be the word 'The' or 'Of.'

Ani DiFranco is an example of a performer who chooses her phrasing and performances more rhythmically. Whether or not she is effective is neither here nor there – it's her style and she is a successful aberration from my little rule

Cover Songs. For performing cover songs, sometimes choosing an action that is totally different from the intention of the song can give you a cool twist on a well-worn song. In my classes, I use the example of Willy Nelson's song "Crazy," which he wrote clearly intending the singer/narrator to be in love with the 'you' of the song, so much that he/she/them is driving the singer 'crazy.' Duh. But say you just can't relate to that, or you want to try to come at it a different way. Who in your life *currently* is driving you crazy? Your sibling? Your mother? Your best friend? Your dog? *What do you want to do to them or get from them?* Well, let's take an example. Say, my sister is driving me crazy (she's not, if she's reading this). She's criticizing me at every turn and I just want to scream at her, but I can't do that because, well, she's my sister. What if I'm holding back a scream? So, I'm singing the song "Crazy" to my sister now and I'm maybe trying to get her to back up? Back off? Do I really want to slap her? That's strong and will produce a completely different tone than the lover pining for the other who drives them crazy.

What if I'm trying to get them to put her arms around me and soften? That is a different tone. You could even play it a bit comedic. Say you're singing to your spouse, someone who you love. But the "crazy" you're feeling isn't because of the love they are giving or withholding, it's because they never clean up. You'd sing the word "crazy" differently—not with any wistfulness, but full of annoyance. That's something the audience wouldn't expect and, also, could lead to some really great banter.

The point is to try different things. Don't just settle for something that doesn't move you while you have to sing the song anyway. Don't get in a performance rut. Try something different.

Those are the most important questions I have for you. I don't want to complicate the matter for you. It's not rocket science. But it's not second nature either, so you do have to do a bit of work on the performance so that there's a journey you're taking the audience on, within your show.

You're in control. That's the main thing. You are never letting go of the reign and they know it and they feel comfortable with you up there steering the horse. Because if they feel your fear, see your anxiety, they're just going to worry about you and then you can't MOVE them. They won't hear your song. They're just nervous FOR you. And if you over perform the song, scooping it out to them like a ham dinner theater actor, jazz-handsing your way through each word with over arched eyebrows and a sad face and listless stares off into the Over The Rainbow distance like a lovestruck teenager, then you're just going to come across like one of those pageant queens, acting each word of the song. If you're in this world of the singer songwriter, they've come to hear truth. Your truth. Their truth. Our truth. BIG TRUTH. Not false tap-dancing sort-of truth. I'd encourage you to be comfortable with looking people in the eye and get really good at sensing when to look away (if you spend the entire song landing each line directly in the eyes of someone, they'll get really uncomfortable). You'll know when the moment has passed. If you're looking at someone and they smile, or they nod, then you move on. If you can't see a soul in the audience, you imagine this.

That said, if you NEVER look at anyone, they'll sense you're freaked out. So try a bit of both. When you have a conversation with a friend, notice how you don't talk constantly at them, looking into their eyes. You're looking around, you're looking up and down, maybe sometimes off to the side, but your attention is still with your friend. Sing your song like that to the audience. Naturally, like it's a conversation between friends.

Serve the physical space of the audience. This is why you walk the stage during soundcheck and check out the perimeters of the audience. When you're performing, you'll look over to the left for a while. You'll serve the right side. You'll serve the back-middle, you'll serve the balcony. You want to create a zone of inclusivity. The 'we are one in this together' feeling. And you do this by looking and connecting with each part of the audience.

Keep your movements and talking slow onstage. Because we naturally speed up when we are up there and it may not seem like it, but you're going two times faster than you think. If you're gesturing, gesture slowly. If you're pointing your arm, stretch your arm out. It's a bit theatrical, but it will seem natural from the audience. If you're telling a story, take your time. Breathe. If you're telling a story, know where the mic is in relation to your mouth so you'll be heard. Be aware of these things. Take your time. Don't let your nerves unbalance you so much that you speed through your intros off microphone and never take a breath before you start playing your intro. Breathe. Especially at the beginning of the show. I take in the audience while breathing, take a beat, then start my song. It's all about breathing.

And, at some point, hopefully, all of this will be second nature to you and will sit in your bones like the technique of scales you practiced all those years while learning to play your instrument, and you will be able to just get up onstage and fly with your songs. Because you have practiced. And when that happens, you'll be hooked. But even the best of us screw up once in a while, and lose track of ourselves up on that great stage, and that's when technique can come in handy. And that's when you now know to ask yourself:

Who are you talking to?
What are you trying to do *to* them or get *from* them?

Chapter Three

TECHNICAL DETAILS

I want to be clear about the method that I teach for you to connect to your song and the audience. This is homework. It's a technique to try out, sometimes with an empty chair and a good imagination, at home. I swear, an empty chair can serve as your mother, lover, friend if you give yourself over to the work. That way, you'll have this work in your body. It will help while you're standing there backstage or in the wings, waiting to go on. You know your first song. Why think about the size of the audience, get lost in stage fright, when you can return to the two questions:

Who are you talking to?
What are you trying to do *to* them or get *from* them?

It works when you get nervous tuning. You remind yourself, "Who am I talking to?" and you look out at the audience and imagine them out there (or, pick someone in the audience who can stand in for that person). This will immediately connect you. It works when you drop a line, screw the guitar part up. Rather than apologize and lose your power—stop, reset yourself and go through these questions in your mind.

If you have a handle on this work, if you have experienced it in your body, I swear you won't forget it. And onstage, for the most part you don't even have to think about it. You start with the question, you look out at the audience, you KNOW what you are doing, you are DOING something, not FEELING something, you have CONTROL of the stage. And you fly. One song moves into the other moves into the other and you are in your body and you feel the connection to your audience and they feel the connection to you and it becomes an almost spiritual journey. That is what we are reaching for. That is why we do this. Whether in an open-mic situation or a seventy-five-minute professional set.

Stage techniques are important to know. You practice these so you know them in your skin, just like the method of performance. I will go through them in no particular order.

THE SOUND CHECK

Be on time. The sound person is on your side and wants to help you sound the best you can. Assume the sound person knows what they are doing. Don't get impatient. The best way to walk through a smooth sound check is to know your equipment. I suggest you buy your own mics for sanitary purposes and to be in control of the sound of your voice. Owning your own mics is a pro move.

Different mics have different qualities. A Shure SM58 is a "fits all" mic. Own one. I went to a music store with a friend who is a sound person I'd worked with and tried out a bunch of mics to see (and to have him let me know) which one was best for my voice. SM58 is the standard, the baseline. I bought a Shure 87A because it has a nice high end, which I know I like on my voice. It's a mid-priced mic. A few years later, with more money, I bought a Neuman KMS105 which, so far, is the best mic I've ever owned. I tell the sound person to leave the EQ alone on that mic. It's an incredible mic and when I bring it, sound people know I'm the 'real deal' (Ian Hunter's sound person was not supposed to do my sound on the tour we did in the UK. The house sound person was to do my sound. But Scooby – Ian's sound person - saw me bring in the Neuman and he said, "You're the real thing. I'll do your sound," and did my sound the rest of the tour. Just because of my microphone).

I own a few DI's of my own with EQ. None of my guitars have EQ on the guitar. I like a DI with my own EQ to have control of my guitar sound. From years of doing this, because of the way I play and to contrast with my high voice, I like a bassy sound. I also have to be careful of a low-mid hum. My high end DI is a Grace Designs "Alix." It is one of the best DIs around. I went to their headquarters in Lyons, Colorado, having met Eben Grace at a festival, and tried out a few of their DIs and chose the Alix (because it was more compact in size, and I travel light). I brought my touring guitar and Eben helped me set the EQ to match my guitar. I took a photo of the settings and put that photo in my "Favorites" file on my iPhone. He had a small-bodied guitar that had the same sound properties as my Collings C-10 and we set that

EQ as well. I can tweak the EQ depending upon the size of the room and its particular sound (usually has to do with ceiling height), but I start out with Eben's settings. That way, I'm in control. I have done this with my D'Addario DI/EQ's as well. I have a photo folder on my phone called "Gear."

I toured with a Nanci Griffith's guitar player who kindly set up my guitar and my mic every night and knew "sound person" language. When my voice wasn't right in the mix, he'd say, "duck the 3K." Now, I have no idea what that means, but it was magic. Since then, I tell the sound person, "you may have to duck the 3K" and I always get the sound I want. It's good to have someone in your corner who knows your voice and knows sound.

I also know what I want in the monitor, and I know where I need the monitor or monitors placed. I want to center myself in between and have them facing me, but not too close so that I'm on top of them. I take two steps back from them and that's usually perfect and then I set the mic stand. With one only monitor, I want it on the left side (not sure why but that surrounds me more than my right) and I stand in the center as if I had two monitors. With piano, it's best to have the monitor on the downstage side so that it doesn't bleed out to the audience and 'confuse' the sound. With a grand piano, I don't need the piano in the monitor.

Before we start the sound check, I tell the sound person, "I want a little 'room' reverb (a certain kind of reverb) in the house for my voice and it coming back at me in the monitor." I like reverb in my monitor because I don't like the sound of my voice "dry." I ask them to do the same settings in the piano. At the piano, I'm fine with an SM 87A or whatever the house has. I use the Neuman at the guitar station, as I play guitar seventy-five percent of my show.

If I'm playing with a guitar player or side person, which is rare, I ask for just a bit of their sound in my monitor. For the most part, I can hear them through their amp. Thomm Jutz (who's one of the best guitar players I've ever played with), put the amp to my right side facing me and then mic'd it for the house. With a bit of his guitar in my monitor I was surrounded by his guitar. He plays a lot of ambient sound. I felt like I was in my own world and loved it, but that's Thomm's style. In rehearsal, I know what kind of sound I want from my side person and, if I'm not getting it from them (I usually am, as I use side players who work with songwriters and really LISTEN to the songs, rather than wank all over the song), I ask.

Soundcheck for me is also an opportunity to get comfortable in my body on the stage. I wear the shoes I'll have on for the show so that I can set the mic at the right height. There's nothing that stops the beginning of a show more than the singer readjusting the mic before they begin.

I physically get to know the space in in which I'll be standing as they introduce me. Will I backstage, with an introduction before walking on stage? Will I be onstage, already plugged in a ready to go? Will I be behind a curtain? Are there cables I need to avoid? On the way to my soundcheck, I walk across the stage (in my show shoes) directly to where I'll stand so that I'm comfortable with that walk. I look out to the house, lit up. I look left. Where is the last seat in the front rows, the back rows? I look right. I look to the back. How far away is the back of the room? Where are the exits? If there's a balcony I look up and get used to including that audience. I get to know the audience before it's dark when I will only be able to hear them. If you're playing an intimate show, like a small club, you can do the same thing. If you're playing a house concert, if you don't have a soundcheck, do this on your first song. Get used to where the people are sitting. You want to connect with them.

During the soundcheck I walk out on the stage as I will that night, get my guitar off the stand *without my back to the audience*, walk directly to the mic. I've practiced putting the guitar cable into the guitar without looking at it. This entire time you are looking at the audience, smiling, welcoming them. If you break contact to watch your cable going into the mic, you break contact, lose the connection. I like to walk out onstage turning to the audience and smiling at them, mouthing "Hi".

Your mouth should be a hand-length away from the mic. Do not 'eat' the mic. It makes for a muddy sound. If you are a belter, practice how far away from the mic you should be. Don't go too far away from the mic or your sound will disappear. I cheat right. I don't physically move away from the mic: that's too far. I just lean my head back. My Neumann can take it without overdrive. Again, know your mic. Know the properties of your mic and where your mouth can go – how near, how far back.

My style (and this may not be your style) is to do two songs before talking. I say nothing in the mic before I start the intro to the first song. If it's an iffy sound situation (rarely) and I'm hesitant about the quality of the sound, I will say "Hi" on mic in order to check that my mic is coming through the monitor and I strum my guitar once to make sure I can hear it in the monitor. Mostly, I stand at the mic (making sure everything is set) and I do not say anything. I take a breath looking at the audience (NEVER LOOK DOWN) and begin my song.

After I'm done with the first song, there will (hopefully) be applause. I look up at them and mouth "thank you" away from the microphone. Then I begin my second song. After my second song, I thank them and say, "Hi. I'm Amy Speace from Nashville (if it's a situation that needs an introduction, otherwise I just go into the rest of my spiel)." And I say something. A little story. An anecdote. Lately with my current set, I play the song "There Used to Be Horses" into "Down the Trail." I feel like it's important to mention both songs are from one album, and I have a good story about "Down the Trail" that contextualizes that song without repeating the story of the song. It sets the scene for the kind of artist, the kind of show I do. Both songs are mid-tempo songs. I go from there into "Hallelujah Train," an uptempo gospel song with a big-voiced chorus. It changes the vibe, gets people toe-tapping and sometimes singing along.

I put two ballads together as song five and six, sometimes four and five. At this point, I like to bring them to an emotional space and keep them there for two songs. The second song is one of my signature songs, "The Sea and the Shore." It's a very emotional song and I need to change the tenor of the room after that, so I do an uptempo cover. Lately, I've been doing a Nanci Griffith song, because I have a good story about opening for her and how she inspired my I move to Nashville.

I'm of the school that thinks you can end with any song you like, just not a real emotional one that will leave them crying. You don't have to play your hit last (some artists save that for the encore), or your most uptempo song last. You can do a ballad. It's really up to you and your style. I do "Hymn for the Crossing," which is a funeral song, but it's a lively happy song (yes, it really is). It leads well into my encore, which is a cover of a ballad, called "Kindness," by Ben Glover, who co-write "Hymn" with me.

You don't always get an encore. Read the applause. There's nothing more awkward than going out to do an encore to mild applause. Don't take it personally. People get tired. There are babysitters to relieve. The audience of the singer-songwriter for the most part are older. Two sets or ninety minutes is a lot to ask of them to sit still. Maybe they have to pee. Don't take it personally!

After your last song, step to the side of your microphone and bow, either with just your head or full body. Don't do it behind the microphone. Your body is hidden. I walk off stage sometimes waving and mouthing "Thank you." I head straight to the merch table to say hi to people and to sell my merchandise. If the venue is selling for you, go the table anyway to say hello and thank you and to sign your CDs and Vinyl.

BANTER

I'll be brief about banter, because it really is a personal thing. Please keep it short and don't talk before every song. There are exceptions to this 'rule,' of course. Some artists are GREAT storytellers, comedians, and it's part of their show. I know a few who talk more than they sing and their shows are brilliant. This section has nothing to do with them (or with you if banter is your main *thing*). It's really up the *kind* of show you have. I'm speaking to the majority of singer-songwriter performers here who, like me, have mostly songs and use banter to introduce or close out a song, or provide a bridge between songs.

With banter, choose your moments. Banter should have the same connection to the audience as your song. In banter, you're talking directly to the audience, even looking at people (get used to looking at people in the eye, or if you're in a theater where you can't see anyone but the front row, look out to the orchestra and up to the balcony and imagine you can see their eyes). Talk to them.

I keep a few 'quips' in my pocket. Most of them I have found accidentally by improvising some night on stage. I got laughs or nods, and I remembered the comment and added it to my arsenal. I have stories I've worked on. Some are for specific songs (i.e. the one about "Down the Trail"). Some can be peppered anywhere in the set. The stories NEVER tell the story of the song. Sometimes they don't even have anything to do with the song. They can set the emotional space you want the audience to be in for the next song. OR, they can do the opposite. I tell a funny story before the highly emotional song "The Weight of the World." It actually serves two purposes for me. It tells the story of when Judy Collins sang that song at the Newport Folk Festival and started talking about the writer and was about to say my name when Pete Seeger interrupted her and she started the song without saying my name. There's a punch line. "I'm not angry at Judy. We're fine. But Pete? If I had a hammer...". It always gets a laugh and then I go into the song.

The other purpose it serves is to tell an autobiographical truth: Judy Collins discovered me and changed my career. I want people to know that but I want to avoid the brag. So, I set it within a story. This is a longer piece of banter and it breaks a rule I have: short banter before long songs; long banter before short songs." "Weight" is a 5-minute song. But the story works well, so I broke my own rule. You can too if it works.

The best thing you can do really learn banter is to take an Improv Comedy Class. I'm not kidding. It will help you learn to think on your feet. And to find your own brand of 'funny'.

One of the reasons I don't talk until before the 3rd song is that I want to set the audience in a musical space and those two songs do that. You may choose otherwise. There are no rules. I do suggest NO STORIES BEFORE YOU BEGIN YOUR SHOW. And, as you will read in *Please Don't Say That on Stage*, don't tell the story of the song (if the song doesn't tell the story, it has failed as a song), don't ask the audience how the sound is, don't ask the audience how they are doing (you really don't want them to answer you).

Banter, as I've written above, can introduce a song, or be like a coda at the end of a song. Or it can serve as a bridge. None of this banter has to have anything to do with the song or songs. I use banter, sometimes, to tell a story that relates to the song. I'll tell a funny story about something that seems like a non-sequitur but is sneaky and illuminates something about the song, even if it's not obvious. I have some stories that literally have nothing to do with my songs, but are good stories and work as the bridge between songs. I have stories that tell a part of my story, to introduce more of myself to the audience, but then, I'm a very personal artist. I play myself on stage, so I tell stories from my life. Your banter will reflect you and the kind of show you want to do.

For instrumental breaks, you are working on *Who am I talking to?* Try to know the piece so you don't have to look at your hands. You can from time to time, but for the most part you can look at the audience or above the audience, or to the side of the audience. Looking down breaks the connection. The instrumental is as much a part of the song as the lyric is. Honor it and your work on writing it.

Try to not have every song begin with a G/C, G/C pattern for 8 bars. A lot of singer/songwriters do that and to be honest, it's boring. You can start the song straight off with the first word of the song. That powerful. If you are a good player, start with a hook.

Slow down. Remember, on stage everything goes faster than in practice. If you make a hand gesture, slow it down to half time. Speak slowly. Don't mumble. You've practiced your set. Honor it. Slow. Down.

A final word: practice. Practice your song. Practice the lyrics so you know them and practice the guitar so you don't have to look at your hands. A method of practicing is to play a song all the way through four times. Then walk away. Then go back and practice it four times. Do this every day with a few of your songs. You'll memorize it that way. Believe me.

Know your show so you are free to have fun, connect and fly!

Chapter Four

THE GIGS

This chapter is dedicated to short bits about the kind of venues you may play as a performing singer-songwriter. I write these notes from experience. In my career, I started out, like many of you, playing my songs for a few friends, then I got the courage to play a few open mics in New York City. My first open mic was at The Sidewalk Café in the East Village. It was run by a guy named Lach, who was well-known for starting what he called the "punk/folk" movement. Michelle Shocked was one of the artists in that movement and she started out at The Sidewalk before she became famous (she also went to the Kerrville Folk Festival and actually recorded a record of her songs in Camp Coho, which became my home camp). I remember how terrified I was. And how long the line was. I was there from six to midnight, just to play two songs.

I've played ALL kind of gigs, cafes, bars, hotels, art festivals, nursing homes, a biker bar in Durango, Colorado, a folk festival at a nudist camp, and a rodeo bar in Wyoming with country bands playing on either side of us, and the audience eager to two-step. We just sped everything up and Rich, my guitar player, took long solos. Oh, did I mention the mechanical bull in the background? Yep. The big time! I've played festivals that were my dream, like Glastonbury in England. I've played theaters and small venues. I've played to thousands and to a handful, including the bartender. It's what this job is. I love it despite the ups and downs.

Open Mics

An open mic is where most of us start out. It's a way to try out your material, to practice the songs. Many times, you're waiting in a long line or signing up on a list full of people. I know established artists who show up at open mics to try out new songs, or on off nights when they are in town touring. Be prepared for a long night. Please don't be the songwriter who plays their song and then leaves. It's rude. Stay. Stay to support the other artists. Who knows, you may find a co-writer or a touring partner out of it.

In Nashville, a possibility to be seen if you're an unknown, is to play The Bluebird Café's open mic on Mondays. I did it once, about twenty-five years ago, when I was in town for a National Association of Campus Activities (a college booking convention) conference. I waited all night to play my one song. Nothing happened. Years later, still living in NY, the brilliant artist David Olney had seen me at the Folk Alliance in one of those small bedroom, late night showcases and liked me. He invited me to join him on a 9pm (the coveted) round at The Bluebird Cafe. Because of that, I was "in" and I host the 9pm rounds now. It's a big deal to host those rounds and I never forget David Olney gave me my break. I'll also never forget that the cab driver who got me to the first open mic at the Bluebird was named Shook and he gave me his demo tape, on which was written in pencil, "Shook: The Cab Driver."

Bars and Restaurants

Bars and restaurants are hard gigs. I started out playing them, taking every gig, and realized I would rather die than play in front a large screen hockey game with nobody listening or, worse—requesting Rolling Stones songs. I stopped doing them because my music is intimate and demands a listening audience. I also never learned a ton of cover material. But they are a great way to get your feet wet and make some midweek money. You need to play usually in restaurants for three hours. That means you need a lot of material for a crowd who may or may not have paid to see you. You can slip in your originals here and there and you should. And you can repeat that first set again later in the night, because most likely the crowd will have changed by then. In this show, you are not of service to the audience, your job is simple: Sell More Alcohol. Keep The Bar Patrons Happy. So, play uptempo songs. Don't pull out the 15 verse maudlin train songs.

Coffee Shops

You will have to fight the espresso machine so get used to it and have a few pieces of banter about it. You are in partnership with the barista, so make friends with them. And sell the audience some lattes and lemon squares so the owners and baristas are happy. You'd be surprised at how many people there for a coffee stop and really listen, and then buy your CD and sign your mailing list and become lifelong fans.

Writer's Rounds

These are shows where you're playing with one to three other (usually) artists, sitting on the stage and playing one song each, down the line, then back again. It's a song swap. It's usual for artists to collaborate on these shows. If someone is a great guitar player, you may invite them to play along. Others may harmonize. It's what makes these great shows. The audience loves the interaction among the artists. I usually have an idea of what songs I'd like to sing, but I'll change it up sometimes based on what was played before me. I may not follow a ballad with a ballad, or I may pick a song of mine to respond to the song played before me. I love these shows. Here's a few tips:

When another writer is playing their song, pay attention to them. Don't be looking around at the audience for your girlfriend or buddy. Wherever your attention goes, some of the audience will follow.

If you are a good guitar player/piano player/harmony singer, do not start accompanying someone else's song right away. Listen to the song first before you go in—and do it quietly— preferably after the first verse, after you get a sense of the structure and chord changes of the song. Watch the writer for cues. Are they giving you a nod of *yeah, keep going*, or do you sense a backing off? Some people do not like other's playing along. It screws them up. So don't take it personally. And remember: this is their song, not yours, so listen and give space.

In a "round" that's set up on a stage, with all the artists lined up horizontally in a row (not sure why they call this a round, but they do), I prefer to stand when it's my turn. This really depends upon the vibe of the show. I'm not trying to show off and I don't want to seem like that. Some artists prefer to sit. I sing and play better standing up. When I'm done with my song, I bring the microphone down to seated level in case there's a harmony opportunity. I play The Bluebird Café in Nashville, where the artists form in a circle in the middle of the room with the audience very closely seated all around them. In that instance, I never stand. Everyone sits. It's way more casual. You do what makes you comfortable. But in these shows, you want to do your best, but it's also about each of you, so be generous to your fellow artists. It's not just your show.

House Concerts

House concerts are the bread and butter of the folk circuit for a singer-songwriter. Really, for any act. I know former hit songwriters who are doing house concerts these days. They can be more lucrative than club shows. And mostly, you sell more merchandise. You're playing, many times, for a new audience, who may not have heard of you but trust their host.

There are a few kinds of house concerts.

The established ones. I know house concerts that have built a stage and lights and sound system in their house and host concerts every month. They are more like a concert series. They book way in advance (a year at least) and are very particular about their bookings. Many of them come to Folk Alliance conferences to check out new artists that have a buzz. It is pretty improbable to book these shows without being well-known on the folk circuit, as they tend to book known performers as headliners who can fill the room. If you're a new(ish) artist and they've seen you play live, they may hire you to open. Many of the concert series don't have openers. Many do. This is why you go to the Folk Alliance conferences, play in small hotel rooms, be seen by folks who literally sit in the front with notepads and seem like they're barely paying attention to you, but are (see *The Gigs*, for more on music conferences). It will do you no good to contact them, as they won't book you, honestly, unless they've seen you. So don't. They get a lot of folks who they don't know emailing them, "I'd love to play your series." Those artists obviously haven't researched the playing field. Research the playing field. Before conferences, it is fine to email hosts of concerts (even business people you'd like to connect with) in advance of a conference to invite them to see your showcases. They may. They may not. You're just letting them know you're here in the scene.

Almost all house concerts work, financially, on a deal where the artist gets one hundred percent of the door, which is usually called "the suggested donation." This way, the house concert is not seen as a professional venue and the host legitimately avoids Performing Rights Organization—ASCAP etc—fees and will not be tagged as a business in a residential neighborhood. Most of these concerts don't pay the opener. Some pay about fifty bucks. Take it. It's a chance to be seen and develop both an audience and a relationship with the more successful artist who may have advice or, better, may offer you another opening act with them. Some of these house concerts pay a guarantee (a specific amount of money agreed upon) to the headliner. At some concerts you can make up to $1000 or more at these concerts.

Another kind of house concert, and this is a good one to pursue as a newbie, is the fan generated house concert. In some of my tours, I have a free night, a Friday or a Saturday where a gig didn't come through. Sometimes a Sunday afternoon. I'll put out a notice to my fanbase to say,

House Concert request! I'm coming through Chicago on _____ and does anyone want to host a house concert? It's easy and I can walk you through it.

Many times a fan will host a house concert, love the idea, and start their own series. With those kind of house concerts, the money is a crapshoot. It's their first time and they can't guarantee you how many people show up. Under ten people can be awkward. For me, I ask for a guarantee of people. Twenty-five people at least at a twenty dollar cover (you'll be asking for a ten or fifteen dollar cover because you're new). I created a PDF document explaining how a house concert works for someone who has no idea how to host one but is up for the task. You can do that as well to help your newbie hosts figure out what this whole "House Concert" thing is about.

Be prepared to play completely acoustically. If you're a quiet singer, this kind of show may not be for you as you need to project in a room that's not suited for a concert. Sometimes the host wants to do an outside show. You have to project. In most of the concerts I do, the host has a sound system, which saves my voice. Be prepared to do your own sound, as sometimes the host may have borrowed a system from a friend and not know how to set them up.

For all house concerts, plan to get there a bit early to set up and soundcheck (if there's time). Ask the hosts if there will be food or should you eat before you come (most feed you dinner). They also want to get to know you. Remember, they are doing you a favor by opening their home and allowing you to make a living. Most times the hosts offer you a room to stay in within their house. Many times the party continues after the concert. Take care of yourself. You can hang out or you can excuse yourself. You've just done a show and you may want to save your voice.

Most house concerts have two sets if you're the headliner, in order to have an intermission for you to sell merchandise (don't go hide in your room... hang out...sell your wares) and for the audience to get more to drinks and eat (it's usually a kind of potluck with drinks, appetizers and desserts). If there' s an opener, there's usually a break after the opener. Then the headliner will play a seventy-five to ninety minute show. As the opener, follow the rules I lay out in *The Opening Act*. Be generous: it's not your show.

House concerts are a very special kind of show. You get to meet your audience and talk to them. You get to spend time with your hosts. Some of the house concerts I've done, the hosts have become my good friends. Know this though: it's not really a way to build your audience outside of the house concert scene. Ninety-nine percent of the audience will not come to your club dates. They're loyal to the house concert, they've gotten to know the artists (who come back every few years), they like the comfort of a home, they don't want to drive into the city. So, if you're building your house concert base, it may not translate when you play the venue in town. You need to build both. You can't do PR for a house concert – they fly under the radar and media doesn't pay attention to them. But still, I love doing them.

At my first house concert, I opened for Ellis Paul in Connecticut. I made fifty dollars and played four song songs in twenty minutes. Ellis played a show that was a master class in performance. I learned a lot watching him. We had a great conversation backstage. The next time I saw him was at the International Folk Alliance Conference. He remembered me and invited me to hang out with some luminaries of the folk world. We swapped songs in the hallway and from there, I started playing shows with Cliff Eberhardt and got the attention of a booking agent and some house concert hosts who had gathered around the circle to hear us and were asking "who is the girl?" I was welcomed into the family. It changed the perception people had of me.

You never know.

Take every gig. It's the only way to get better. Don't be better than any gig. Be humble and use the opportunity.

The Clubs/Small Theaters/Big Theaters

This is where you're really doing the thing. You're probably touring. You probably have a booking agent, a manager, maybe even a PR person, a radio promoter, the whole shebang. You could even be on a record label. A lot of times, at this level, you aren't booking yourself, you have a team doing this. But when I started out, I was contacting these small clubs myself. I'd ask for opening shows. I'd build my audience in that area, and I'd get more and more headline shows. Not weekend shows. But the mid-week ones. I'd make sure I did everything I could to promote them to ensure I could bring an audience. That they could *see* that I could bring an audience. Because if you can't, you won't be invited back. Which is why I say wait to do this until you have an audience (unless you're the opening act).

Theaters and clubs are dream gigs for me. Pro sound, pro lighting. A warm audience. Maybe even a dressing room with snacks and tea.

Know this: the performance technique is the same whether you're playing a small club or a big theater (As Judy Collins taught me, the sparkle might change).

It's a small, small world. Be nice to everyone. Including the guy who is an asshole and yells "Play a train song." He's probably drunk, so keep a few "Yeah, I can remember my first beer" kind of quips in your back pocket, but don't say them to shame that person. And learn a train song. It'll come in handy in those moments.

If people are talking, there's a lot of noise, you feel like you're losing them, don't get louder, get softer. In fact, get as soft as you can get and then step off the mic and keep singing. Someone will shush them, or they will turn around to find out what's going on. It's the kindest way of telling an audience to shut the fuck up. And it works.

Only in the rarest of circumstances can you berate an audience, or even one rude person. You risk making everyone uncomfortable. Allow the other patrons who are listening to you to help quiet them down. When enough is enough, gracefully ask that person to take their conversation elsewhere so that everyone else can enjoy the show. That goes for any phones that go off. Get used to it. People forget. Keep going. I've had people start to carry on a conversation on their cell phone during a ballad. What do I do? I come off mic and put my attention on them until they notice and stop talking. Or I'll unplug, keep playing, walk to their table and sing straight to them. Or I'll just stop and make a directed piece of banter that's sharp but funny, "Hey if it's for me, tell them I'm busy." They'll stop. And if they don't, someone will stop them. Don't pull a diva and let that derail you. It's still your show.

As a performing artist starting a career (and even well into one), you'll most likely play all of these gigs. If you know covers and can pull off playing for three hours, that's a good side job. I have a dear friend who's a brilliant writer and is just starting off getting notice from the folk world. She makes a living playing The Hyatt and The Hilton and corporate gigs. And, bonus, she can pepper her set full of covers with her original songs. I can't do that. When I needed a day job, I was a legal secretary. I can type really fast.

Don't quit your day job until you can quit your dayjob and make a living playing shows. Not many can and they quit because they can't pay their rent. Why not stick with your job, make your money, and do regional tours on weekends? You won't get a booking agent until you have a buzz and it's worth paying fifteen percent of your incoming money to take you on. Same with managers for the most part. Unless you have a friend with a killer business sense who wants to manage you. Josh Ritter's manager is his college roommate and they've done pretty well together.

In conclusion, play every opportunity you can get. It's good practice and you'll learn how to play for all kinds of audiences. And you may even get a few folks at The Hyatt to buy your CD and come see you when you play a singer-songwriter venue in town.

Chapter Five

THE OPENING ACT

A rite of passage for all aspiring singer-songwriters is to be invited to be the opener to a headliner at a club or a house concert. This could be a great opportunity to make new fans, to be heard by the club/house concert so that someday you'll get the headlining gig yourself, and to be heard by the headliner so that maybe they'll as you to do more shows with them. Most house concerts won't even book you until you've passed through as an opener a few times.

When you are the opener, always remember: **THIS IS NOT YOUR GIG**. It is the headliner's, and your job is to warm up the room for the headliner. You are borrowing their stage and their audience and you must act with grace and a modicum of deference at all times. And believe me, I've screwed up most of these 'rules', which is how I figured it out. And it was not the artist who kindly and gently let me know. Once it was the tour manager, who told me if I didn't come in UNDER my thirty-minute time the following night (for a major artist), I would not be allowed back. Take it from me. You want to learn this stuff.

You sound check AFTER the headliner, so never load in your gear onstage until it has been made clear that the headliner is done (by the headliner or the sound person). You may arrive earlier than the headliner. You sit and wait your turn, unless someone gives you the go ahead (like the headliner is running late and it may be more time effective for you to soundcheck first). I've seen openers set up their pedals and gear onstage off to the side while the headliner is sound checking—or worse, sit in the audience noodling on their guitars, tuning, changing strings, basically making noise during soundcheck.

Not only will they never get the gig again, most likely they will not get the gig with anyone that headliner (or their agent or their manager) know. Believe me, I've sat at a table with a bunch of high ranking artists who share names

If we're talking about the Folk/Americana world, unless told otherwise, play solo acoustic if you are a solo artist and can do that, or at least in a configuration that takes up the least amount of space and means very little stage changeover. If you are mostly a solo artist, but prefers performing as a duo or trio or full band, always ask whomever it is has booked you and get an ok before you go hiring the full enchilada. When I perform, whether I'm solo or duo or full band, I want a solo artist to open for me. More than one person takes up too much room and time.

Also, I don't want something louder than me to go on before me. I have been invited to open for large bands in huge theaters and I've performed with a full band, but only after asking if that's appropriate. If you are performing with a full band to open for a major act, ask if there will be someone doing your sound or should you bring your own soundperson. Most major bands travel with their own sound/lighting people and won't be doing your sound. Don't get stuck. Ask.

Stay *under* your allotted time. If you have been given thirty-minutes, play for twenty-five. **Do not, under these circumstances, go to thirty-five or forty**. This is the most egregious error. It really pisses off everyone involved. You will not be invited back. Time your set with your banter to be sure you come in on time.

Don't talk too much. You will exhaust the audience that is there to see the headliner and most likely will be thinking "why won't this person shut up and play the song." If you are opening for a songwriter, play only *one* cover song, at most, if any. The audience is geared to wanting to hear original songs. Too many covers bores the audience. Plus, you want to sell your CD, right?

If you are sharing the merch table with the headliner, wait until they set up their own display and take up as little room as possible. Again: it's their show. Set up one (maybe two) CD, one t-shirt and your mailing list. Do not put out your catalogue of five CDs, an EP, a poster, four T Shirts, your keychains and tote bags and special home-made jewelry and knitted hats. It's. Their. Show.

Thank the headliner from the stage. Even if they are nowhere to be seen. It's gracious. And should be obvious but I've seen the blunders.

Never take an encore, UNLESS the headliner gives you permission. Like when the audience is wildly applauding, and the headliner is listening from the wings and waves you to take an encore. Then go for it. (This happened to me when I opened for Nanci Griffith at Town Hall in New York City. I played for twenty-five minutes. She listened to me from the wings. Talk about a generous headliner).

Otherwise, let the audience stomp on the floor in a rousing standing ovation while you, generously and graciously, bow and leave the stage for the headliner and make it clear that you are done. That is egoless and that is behavior that will be rewarded with another gig. And after such a rousing ovation, you'd better head straight to that merch table and collect your $2,000 in 20 minutes.

Assume the headliner isn't even going to listen to you and do not take it personally when they don't. They're touring. You are most likely local. They've been sleeping in motels for a month straight, just drove six hours and did two radio interviews and they are exhausted. That half an hour in the green room to meditate or go over their set list or eat dinner while you're playing is a rare gift for them. But if you do see them after your set or after their own, do not ask "Did you see my set?" just thank them for having you and give them their space. Don't be a gurm.

Learn a few of the headliner's songs. Find out what they usually close the show with or what their encore songs are. Learn their hit. Learn the harmony. Learn the guitar part. They may just invite you up to sing with them. Be prepared if they do. Know the lyrics. I've been invited up so many times. I'm glad I learned my lesson only once, but it was a hard lesson to learn because at at a sold out show of 900 people, Nanci Griffith invited me up to sing "Flyer" with her and I was stupid and didn't know it. Duh. Opportunity lost.

If you are invited to share a dressing room with the headliner, never ever take up much room in the room. Never eat the food from their food tray without their permission – that might be their dinner. And never invite your buddies or parents to come hang out and eat from the food tray if it is not your own dressing room. Again: Not. Your. Show.

Send thank you notes/emails to anyone involved with the show. The headliner. Their manager and/or agent. The club owner/promoter/booker. Then troll their sites and see if there are any other dates that do not have openers announced and ask the manager/booking person/artist directly if they'd consider you for those dates.

Lastly, a point about money. I've had opening slots that paid me $700 and I've had opening slots that paid me nothing. I've had opening slots that I had to pay for (paying into the Major Artist's tour's advertising budget for my name on the poster). The usual for a singer-songwriter is zero dollars to $100 with fifty being the most likely. If you are good and well-matched with the headliner, you will sell CD's as to the audience you will be a discovery.

When I opened for Nanci Griffith, playing to 900 people who'd probably paid almost fifty dollars a ticket. I was offered nothing for the show. I took it. I did an opening tour for Ian Hunter on his UK Acoustic Tour in 2009 for nothing. I lost a lot of money on that tour, as I had to pay my own flight, travel, hotel. I sold CD's, and I sold a lot. And Ian would invite me up at the end of the night to join the band in "All The Young Dudes" (not bad for a folk singer) and he ended up singing on a record of mine and has become a bit of a mentor for me. But even more than that, every time I go back to the UK to play, a handful of huge Ian Hunter fans come to my shows. I keep getting dividends from that money-losing tour so many years ago.

So how do you get an opener? Relationships, mostly. Being a fan. I made (sometimes still do) lists of artists that are up on the food chain a few rungs from me, who were playing larger theaters than I was playing and I asked my manager and agent to submit me as opener for tours. When I was starting out and I was my own manager and booking agent, I'd troll certain artists' websites to find out where they were playing and I'd figure out my six degrees of separation between them or their manager or agent (usually listed on their websites) or the promoter or booker of the club itself. I'd write people, send a very brief email, VERY Brief, like as in three sentences. I'd attach a LINK to my music, not an mp3 (clogs up their inbox, super rude), and a link to my website. I'd make some reference that would make them want to read the email. Maybe a referral from a mutual acquaintance or artist.

Dear Martin Sexton,

I was just doing a festival with your sister Colleen last week and she mentioned I should get in touch with and ask you about opening for your upcoming show at the Narrows Center for the Performing Arts on May 29th. I'm from the area and have a good draw at [local area club], where I recently sold out a show and would love the opportunity to play the Narrows. Below is a link to 3 of my songs and a link to a Youtube video of my show [if you're pitching a solo opener don't send them a video of you and your band].

I'm a huge fan and appreciate your time,
Joe Schmo"

If I got that email, I'd take the time to listen to the music and watch the video. The headliner may get busy and forget to answer. Feel free to follow up a week or two later, really briefly. If they don't answer after that, don't take it personally, take it as a no for now and move on. Or contact the venue directly. Or contact their manager or agent. Be persistent but don't be a pest. There are great clubs that I play that I know I cannot fill, but the booker there (and by now the manager, the sound people, the staff) are really supportive and know I can do a good opening job, so I troll the website a few months out and pitch myself directly. If the booker says "yes, check with the artist's management" and I can't find the management info easily, I'll ask the club booker for that person's email and I'll write directly the same kind of email above. Brief and to the point with backup material, but not too much. And then I'll follow up with a phone call.

The thing is this: the headliner may not want an opener. It just makes the night longer, so what do you offer them? Think about it. Are you good for a few tickets? Can you ingratiate yourself honestly into their lives so that you can act as tour manager/driver AND opening act. Can you back them up as a sideperson or harmony singer on some songs AND be an opener? Be of service to an artist you respect and they will want you out there onstage with them. They'll be thrilled to help you out. Someone helped them. Most artists want to pay it forward. And if they don't, forgive their narcissism and move on with a smile.

Again, remember another golden rule: TAKE NOTHING PERSONALLY.

Chapter Six

PLEASE DON'T SAY THAT ONSTAGE

What separates the wheat from the chaff, the pro from the amateur? Pro's exhibit an ease and comfort in their stagecraft, how they move on stage, how they handle their instrument, their voice, their phrasing, the in-between song stories and banter. Pro's let mistakes slide and sometimes use them to their benefit. Amateurs apologize. Pro's move on.

Here are a few things to avoid saying onstage at all costs:

"This song is about..."

Listen up: if you have to explain what the song is about, you haven't written a good song. Period. Try to avoid over-explaining what you're about to sing, because you are setting yourself up for failure. If you tell the audience what they are about to hear, you encourage them to decide line by line on whether you have successfully written a song that is about what the song is about. Get me? Instead, choose some anecdote from your life, a funny story, a true story, an observation that shines a light on the thing inherent in your song you want them to get. Is it a love song about two people who never match up? Share something about one of your relationships or something about a friends'. Or your parents. Or your grandparents. Ships passing kind of thing. Then NEVER DRAW THE LINE FROM THE BANTER TO THE SONG, ALLOW THE AUDIENCE TO DO THAT. Just transition from story into song without the explaining phrase "and so, I wrote this song about that kind of love...". You've killed the cool thing about the story. And that bores an audience. It's theater. Allow for magic.

Other banter options will be discussed later, but seriously, leave out the "this song is about" crap. And yes, I know, you've heard pro's do this over and over, but I guarantee the banter would work way better if the pro left that out.

"How many songs do I have left?" or "How much time do I have?"

(usually accompanied by shading eyes with your hand and scanning the audience for the sound person)

This breaks the fourth wall and lets the audience know you are not in control. Time your sets so you know how long they are. Cut stories. Cut songs. This goes for the headliner as well.

If you are the headliner, be aware of the club's curfews. Say your show is advertised to begin at 8:00pm, you don't go on until 8:20 or so, you do two sets, your intermission stretches a bit while you say hi to your fans and family and sell CD's, you go back on to do another forty-five minute set, but you stretch it out to sixty minutes and then you get a few encores. If the club is ok with this, you're golden. But say you're playing a bar or a restaurant and you notice the folks who work there cleaning up and generally standing around waiting for you to be done...then wrap it up. Because every person working that night from the sound person to the waiters serving the tables to the bartenders to the door people really don't care about your music. They are watching the clock to see when they can finish up their own night and get back to their boyfriends, girlfriends, kids, Netflix, etc. Just be aware of time and don't go too much over.

It's always better to leave the audience wanting more (they'll be excited about the next time you come through town!) then risking them feeling awkward about leaving toward the end, not knowing when will be done (they'll have negative associations with you and will skip your next show).

"I tune because I care" or any other comments/jokes while you're struggling tuning

Just shut up and tune the damn guitar. It will go much much faster. Besides, the world has heard all of the tuning jokes. The best tuning banter I've heard is from Judy Collins, who struggles sometimes with keeping her 12 string guitar in tune – critical for her, as she works with a piano player. When it's taking her a bit longer, Judy will say "Back in the day I learned a lot working with Ravi Shanker. He made tuning into a religious experience." Bam. If you can't be that witty, then just tune and move on.

Any kind of apology

"I have this cold. Usually my voice is much better." Apologizing for your guitar playing. "This is the first time I've ever played this song, so I hope I don't screw it up." The more you point out your potential flaws the more your audience will look for them. Some flaws are charming. Some are just mistakes and will end the spell you've put your listener under during the song. Own your flaws, but don't tell us about them.

A word on screwing up: this can be a golden moment in a performance. The most riveting performer is doing a high wire dance between practiced grace and perfection and the possibility of the fall. We love to watch them balance, lose their balance momentarily, and then readjust and get it back. It's the heart-stopping moment. So if you forget a line to a song, or you screw up a chord, or you miss a vocal note, learn to allow it, acknowledge it, and readjust. The audience will forgive you and may lean in closer.

I remember a Dar Williams show I saw years ago where she forgot the words to a song and kept playing the guitar while talking, "I've totally lost the second verse, um, does anyone out there know it?" and some audience member started singing the words to her. Dar basically nodded to that person and invited them onstage to sing the whole verse. The audience applauded wildly. She was gracious, she was truthful, she didn't pretend it didn't happen but allowed for the mistake and improvised. A perfect rebalancing act. She tripped and got back on the high wire. Allow. Say "yes and", not "no but" to these moments. If you have them in your town, I highly recommend taking Improv Comedy classes. This will quickly teach you these skills of quick recovery. Of thinking on your feet.

Chapter Seven

THE SUGGESTION BOX

I dare you...

I dare you to jump in and just do it. By "do it," I mean think of yourself as an artist. Some of you want to do this for a career. Some of this have careers and want to be weekend warriors. Some of you are happy playing these songs for your family. Whether or not you ever make a dime out of your music, or get to a national stage, you are still an artist and I'm still going to push you to get your music out there by singing it in front of people.

Stop telling me why you haven't, why you can't. Stop telling me you're not good enough, that THEY are better. Stop listening to the people from your past who said "No" to you...

Here's the thing: You are an Artist. You know it and now I know it. So, stop listening to the NO, both in your head and out there, and lean into the YES.

It's only you who are stopping yourself. The truth? I know you want to, and the world *really really really* needs you to, too.

And here's why. YOU are the only YOU. It's really that simple.

There is no one else that can do what you do, say what you say, sing like you sing, write what you write. The world needs YOU. The world also needs Taylor Swift. And Mary Oliver. And Mary J. Blige. And the dude who sings off-key at the open mic every Monday. And that girl who won the songwriting contest (who you know in your darkest of hearts *totally* didn't deserve to win and clearly you were robbed). The world needs her too. Stop worrying about what everyone else has or doesn't have and get to work on making sure you are completely the best YOU possible.

Because <u>we need you</u> (have I said it enough?). The best YOU can change the world. The comparing, complaining, making-excuses you? Yeah, we don't need that person that much. They bore the pants off the world. We want the God or Goddess You. The Highest Form of You. The Buddha You. The Ghandi You. The Mick Jagger You. The Oprah You. The Michelle Obama You. The loud you. The grand you. The quiet you. The HONEST you.

Make a study of You. Be fascinated by You. That is <u>not</u> to say be *self-centered*. Far from it.

BE SELF-INTERESTED AND OTHER CENTERED

This you? The "God You"? Yeah, the world doesn't give a shit how old you are, how much you weigh, if you wear the latest trends, that you started late or missed your big chance, or this is your first song or your hundredth. As long as you are telling the truth. Then the world is gonna fall madly in love with you. I guarantee it.

STAGE FRIGHT IS A CON

Stage Fright is Fear. Fear is Darth Vader. *Purpose* is Luke Skywalker. Fear is not as strong as Purpose, so Purpose will ALWAYS defeat Fear. But the trick is that Fear has better costumes than Purpose so we get a bit sidetracked by its tomfoolery. Fear masks itself as anger, as jealousy, as ennui, as procrastination, as excuses, as exhaustion. But Purpose? Purpose has legs, purpose has intention, purpose knows what to do and when in doubt, purpose just improvs, makes a quick choice and wings it with elan and humor. <u>And Stage Fright disappears when Intention shows up</u>. Here's the thing. We get scared when we stand on stage or get up in front of anyone to share our art and we worry about OURSELVES. The voice in our head gets louder. "You suck" "You didn't practice" "Why bother?" "You definitely look awful in those jeans" ...

CONFIDENCE AND STAGE PRESENCE

We all see other people we deem confident and we either try to beat them out with bravado or we shrink a bit, thinking they were born with this. Same with "stage presence" (the ineffable quality that critics seem to use to divide those who have and those who have not). Here's the thing. Yes, there are people that are born with a kind of glow. How they got it is beyond me. Maybe I have it (I know I have it when I am onstage). Maybe you have it and don't know. Maybe neither of us has it and we're just hard workers. There are those. They say Taylor Swift had it to begin with, but none of us knew her as she was practicing as a young child at talent shows. Maybe she was awkward and didn't glow. And then just did it over and over and over again until she emerged, after the record deal and the grooming, with Stage Presence. Maybe she was born with it. Why compare? I know people who seem to have come out of the womb writing great songs. They're otherworldly, lucky creatures to me. I know people that started out as *meh* songwriters and worked hard and became great songwriters.

Augusten Borroughs, in his incredible book *This Is How,* writes that confidence cannot be bought or taken as a pill. It's basically (and I'm trying to directly quote him but I'm not sure I am, but I do know the curse is in there), "the ability to not give a shit about what others think of you". It's not our business. We do our work, we do our best, and come what may what the critics say.

If I can walk onstage *knowing that I worked at my intentions and my playing and on the song until I'm doing the best work I can*, then I don't have to worry about what other's think of me. And if I can wrap my head around that, then THAT'S confidence. And confidence plays a role in stage presence. It may even sum it up. I heard a woman say that stage presence was 'bringing your best version of yourself to the stage'. I like that. But again, *how* do you do that?

I'd say, unless you're Lady GaGa, BE yourself. But expand so that you're not just the you going to the grocery store. You're the you, yes, with confidence, who knows if you're up there doing your work (that you've practiced), and your intention is .... What???...to connect, honestly, truly that your intention, then you'll have stage presence. The lack of stage presence, which may help you understand, is fear.

INTENTION SILENCES THE NEGATIVE VOICES IN OUR HEADS

First things first: this job is not ego-centered (and by job I mean the "job" of sharing our art with someone else, whether that's your boss, your grandchildren or your audience of people who paid to see your show). It is a service position. We are mere bartenders and bag-fillers at the grocery store here. "How are you doing? Are you having a good night? What can I get you?" Are you *really* talking to your audience or are you just pretending to care about them? Look at them. Talk TO them. Not *over* them. Don't just flit your eyes across the first row nervously, hoping they don't see how freaked out you are. They will. Always. But they will forgive if you acknowledge the fear as a fellow flawed human being on a shared journey.

And they will not leave. The audiences crave connection. They want YOUR attention, maybe more than you want theirs. Give them your attention. When you look at 'the audience', really LOOK AT THEM. Look at one person at a time. Not for too long, but for enough time that you exchange some kind of moment (If they don't look at you or they look away, accept that as the 'moment' that you shared, and then you move on. Acknowledge the "what is" rather than grieve the "what it could have been." By the way, this is really good advice given to me by a good friend about relationships in general). Here's the thing—you will feed the fear if you DON'T really look at people, grazing your eyes quickly across the audience in general. What I call "Focus Flitting". That says to them, "I'm terrified and I hope you don't notice me." Really looking at them and landing on them says, "I've GOT this!" Focus calms them, and then calms you.

Next: when you are performing your songs, *offer* them the songs, the intention of the song itself. What is the song about? To whom are you singing the song? What do you need for yourself or what does the person you are singing to need? Really OFFER the song to the people in front of you, don't just stand up onstage mumbling, belting, over-singing or rushing your words. Have respect for the audience, for their time, for the money they have paid to see you or, at the very least, the things they gave up (TV, laundry, a movie, dinner, sitting at the bar talking to the hottie) to sit in this seat while you are up there performing. Talk to them not at them. Have intention. Make connection.

RESPECT YOUR AUDIENCE

This is "show business." If someone is paying money to see you or paying TIME to see you, respect their investment and honor it with gratitude. The job of the performer is sacred and it is a service position (see above reference to bartenders and bag checkers -- I'm not kidding). We are here to serve the audience, not our egos. As much as you think that the big stars are ego-filled narcissists (and yes, some of them are) the BEST ones are the ones who connect and care a whole damn lot about you. Yes, they do. Or else you wouldn't keep buying tickets to their shows. So, respect your own audience's loyalty. Dress the part. Clean up. Don't wear a baseball hat on stage backwards or flip flops, unless that's part of your thing. Tune your guitar. Know the lyrics to your songs. You don't have to doll up like a Vegas showgirl but be better than your everyday "I'm just getting the morning paper in my sweatpants-self. With the show itself- don't 'wing it'. Be prepared.

WRITE A SET LIST

Write a set list at least an hour or so before the show and visualize the arc of the show, banter and songs included. Bring it on stage and have it at your feet or taped to your guitar or on the stool next to you so you can see it (and check to make sure the spotlight hits the setlist – another thing to do during soundcheck is to ask to see the stage lights so you know where the light hits the things you need to see). I hate writing set lists. But I love that I have them when I get derailed. At the very least, know the first two songs and the last two songs and if you lose your place somewhere in the middle because the sound goes out or the lights flicker or you forget a chord and that critical voice in your head gets loud, I hope you will remember that a set list would have helped you get the train back on the tracks.

If you are on the track to doing this professionally, I suggest keeping a dated file of your setlists. When I return to a venue, I look at the setlist from the previous show to make sure I'm not just repeating the same set again, a year later. (I hear Emmylou keeps notes on her lists as well, like what she wore to the show, so she doesn't show up a year later in the same outfit so that the photographs don't betray her. GREAT idea!). The set list will help keep you in control because...

YOU ARE THE CONDUCTOR OF THIS RIDE

Your job is to take the audience on a journey that you've mapped out. When you enter the stage walk to the microphone and pick up your guitar, do it with the purpose and intention and deliberation of a craftsman picking up their tools and sharing those tools lovingly with people who you respect and like. Do not grab your guitar haphazardly, slapping on your capo sideways, banging into the microphone stand. Be in a state of gratitude and service throughout the show. No matter what happens. The audience will trust you if you are trustworthy. Keep both hands on the wheel.

Conductors know their equipment and know the route and don't rush. Everything on 'stage time' goes way faster than you think, so to practice, try to do everything at 'half time'. Slow everything down.

Try to not talk into the microphone during the applause. Let the applause ride its natural wave, and as it's dying down, then begin to speak. Too many performers make this mistake and their intro's and thank you's get lost in the applause. If you are thanking someone, say the sound person or the promoter, you want the audience to hear their name. Have patience. They will wait for you. You do not have to rush. This is a very hard thing for newbie performers, who feel like they want to get it done and get out of the way. It's quite the opposite. If you are holding my attention, I'm in for the ride and I'll go where you want me to go. So, take your time and be the conductor of a train that you control. Don't be the conductor who's racing after the runaway train.

THE PERFORMANCE BEGINS THE MINUTE YOUR FOOT HITS THE STAGE

Your walk across to the microphone is as important as the first note. That interminable time before you sing? The audience is waiting for you. Walk slowly, acknowledge the audience (a little smile or a nod will do), and take your time. Plug your guitar in. Check to make sure everything is working, check to make sure the mic is still at the correct height (if you did not do your soundcheck in your 'show shoes' you may be taller now in your heels. Get your mic where you need it). Take a breath. Then start the song. Don't start your instrumental while you are getting your feet steady as the audience won't know that you've begun and it will feel like you are creeping your way into the song. Imagine an old school film clapper. "Rolling". Imagine that moment and THEN you can start the song.

BREATHE

BREATHE

BREATHE

Unlock your hips so your channel is open. Bend your knees. Make sure you're balanced. If you're not, get into yoga, walking, swimming, meditation. Performing is a sport. Be in shape.

BE CLEARHEADED SO THE MUSE
CAN COME OUT TO PLAY

Don't be fooled by drugs and alcohol. You may think it makes things flow easier on stage. And I don't mean to be a fuddy-duddy. But that stuff gets in the way of the cosmic spiritual flow which makes a great performance a great performance. You don't want your ability to adapt and improvise to be impaired. If you're Todd Snider or another artist where a kind of smoky hazey improve trippy performance is your "Thing", well, be my guest, good luck to you, and it might be great and it might be a train wreck and maybe it's worth the $50. Respect your audience and show up to work on time and straight. I love what Janis Ian writes about this:

Alcohol and drugs don't eliminate stage fright; they just bury it where you can't be affected until you fall into the hole they've made. Far better to actually rid yourself of the monkey on your back.

DID I MENTION BREATHING??

When you're stuck, breathe. When you're nervous, breathe. When you forget a line, breathe. Unlock your knees, wiggle your hips and breathe. Fear locks us up, physically, psychically and emotionally. Breathing is the antidote to fear. Real breathing. Not just shallow from the neck up breathing, but deep from the depths of your gut and the bottom of your ass as if your feet were old roots from a Sequoia that attached through the soil through the clay and rock to the center of the earth where God lives. Breathe that deeply and you will breathe with God. Who has time for stage fright when you are channeling that kind of energy?

GRATITUDE

On the set list, write down the name of the sound person, the host, the promoter, your opening act, and anyone who made the show possible. And thank them. By name. You'd be surprised how much that means to them. And to the audience who will have the chance to applaud and thank them for having you. You have no idea how much power a sound person wields. Stay on their good side. Even if they suck.

Sound people are generally underpaid and love music, and most are musicians who play in bands too. And sometimes they are recording engineers, and they love to play with your sound during the show and add reverb in the middle of the song "Monster monster monster Truck truck truck...". If you don't like that, (and I don't) then know what you want and ask for it during soundcheck and let them know you prefer them not to change things too much once you get going.

I walk into the sound check and introduce myself and my players to everyone and then I let the soundperson know exactly what kind of sound I prefer in the house AND in the monitors. I carry my own mic. I spent time with a sound person checking out what frequencies are problematic with that mic and with my particular voice, so that I can speak "soundperson language" and not just say "um, the sound is strange". I can be more specific. I also have my own DI and EQ on my guitar ,and I know how I want the guitar to sound.

It might not be how the sound engineer wants it to sound, but it's how I want it to sound and so I let them know what I want for my show in a very professional but polite way.

If you like reverb, figure out what kind because "room" sounds different than "slapback" or "theater" and know if you like it coming back at you in the monitors or not. I like a dry guitar sound and a "small room" reverb with a short tail on my vocals. I know what that means and so does my sound person. I know that in some rooms, if there seems to be a low-mid "Hoof" sound in my voice, I ask the engineer to duck the 3K. I also know I like a lot of room on my voice in the high's, but I also use reverb and a pretty high-endy mic, so sometimes I get an "S" sizzle that's too much and it's a dance between ducking the high's and ducking the reverb. You'll learn by doing and by asking.

And if I'm in the middle of the show and things have gone south, I allow myself one moment of "hey can I have more of ..." with my sound person, maybe two, if it's really bad. More than that and the audience starts to know that something is afoot and then their attention is on the sound and not the show. And you will lose them. Sometimes you gotta just go with the flow. Never berate the sound person from the stage though on microphone. Never. Ever. Ever. And never ever ever ask the audience 'How does it sound" because that's an insult to the underpaid, hard working, fellow tribe member sound engineer

A FEW LAST WORDS

Sleep is really critical. So is water. So, for me, is Throat Coat Tea. So is warming my voice up. So is getting to the venue on time to be a good worker bee and also give yourself some time to chill and get focused. Make sure you don't wear a belt buckle or a bedazzled shirt or a piece of jewelry like a necklace that click against the back of the guitar during the show. Practice in your stage outfit, your stage shoes. Write out your banter and practice it and then cut it shorter and practice again until you know it and can improvise it. Even if you only have two songs to do. Practice those two songs and your 'hello' introduction and what you'll say in between as if those two songs are your full show. This is a good practice for those of you who audition or get to showcase at music conferences or enter contests. Make those two songs or that 1 song a Great Performance. Not just an apology for what you could do if you were given thirty minutes. And don't tell me "I need a few songs to warm into my show." You don't have three songs to warm into your show. You have the time you walk across the stage to grab your guitar. Bruce Springsteen starts his show as if that first song is his encore and then goes for 3 hours, each song is the encore. It's exhilarating.

Make each time you perform meaningful to both the audience and you. Enjoy the sound of your own voice, but don't *listen* to yourself. Allow. Loosen the grip. And then fly...

I dare you-

Chapter Eight

THE LAST CHAPTER (WHEREIN I'M NOT SURE HOW TO WRAP THIS THING UP)

At this point, I think I've given you all I know, all I've learned in my twenty plus of being a performing singer-songwriter. I cut my teeth in the competitive world of New York City and learned how to hear "no" over and over. I learned how to keep going and sometimes, later, that "no" turned into a "yes." I went to every music conference I could to learn about the business (I spent a lot of money, but it was an investment in my career). I'd get up early and be the geek in the front row of the radio panel with questions prepared. I'd go up to the panelists and introduce myself. I wouldn't hand them a CD because (this I learned from my music business friends) they don't want to take a CD home. Of course, this is old information now that nobody has a CD player. Instead, have a card with your Spotify link and only give it to them if they ask. I learned this from the music business friends after being privy to their conversations after some eager songwriter approached them at the bar with their CDs. Those CDs were thrown out.

I entered all the contests. It took years, but finally I had a season of being a finalist in every one of them and even winning a few. I went to the International Folk Alliance Conference (because I'm a folk singer) for five years before anyone noticed me. It was worth it. I got House Concerts and festivals and a booking agent there. I moved to Nashville to be more a part of the songwriting center of the world and it has made me a better writer. I went to songwriting camps and sat at Darrell Scott's feet and learned to write better and better songs.

Basically, I learned to make friends with rejection and keep going. Because I knew I had something to offer. I knew my Joan Baez-esque voice wasn't out of time, it was unique. I kept at the songwriting until I started writing good songs. I've written a few that have won awards. Twenty years into my career.

I learned to tour the hard way. By booking myself and taking no money and losing money and sleeping on couches. It was a master class in performance. When I got home from my first seven-week tour across the country, I can honestly say I was good.

I just kept at it. Because I knew. Deep down in my gut I knew something. That I could do this thing. Now, listen. I'm not famous. I haven't won a Grammy. But if you're in the Folk or Americana world, chances are you've heard of me. I didn't get into this to be famous. I got into this to live amongst artists and make a living at what I created. Even if I never made a living at this and had to take another job, I'd still write songs and make records and do shows. I just got lucky. But I persevered and knew where I was strong and knew where I was weak and worked hard.

It takes losing money. It takes working hard. It takes moving to a music center (it really does, sorry to say, living in the middle of Wyoming is not going to help your music career). And most importantly, in the end, it's about the SONG. Write a great song and it will change your life.

And since this is a book on performance, once you've written that song, learn to perform it honestly. Learn to connect. Get to the place where people come up to you and tell you how they related to your music. That's winning. That's better than fame.

Why not? What have you got to lose? You're an artist, remember. Always remember that. And remember, I'll be here cheering for you.

ABOUT THE AUTHOR

Amy Speace is an internationally-acclaimed singer and songwriter, teacher, workshop leader and author. She has taught workshops in performance for over twenty years at The Rocky Mountain Folks Festival Song School. She has also taught at Berklee College of Music, University of Colorado, Denver, The Kerrville Folk Festival Song School, The Swannannoa Gathering and many more. She also leads her own retreats called "Songs From The Well" in Tennessee. She has been published in *The New York Times*, *Salon*, *No Depression*, *Performing Songwriter* and *Blurt*. Her poetry has been published in *2River Review* and *Euonia*. She holds an MFA in Creative Writing (poetry) from The Naslund-Mann School of Writing at Spalding University, a Certificate in Acting from The National Shakespeare Conservatory and a BA from Amherst College in English and Theater Studies from Amherst College. She lives in Nashville, Tennessee.

Made in the USA
Columbia, SC
10 September 2024

42067232R00043